**HARVARD MIDDLE EASTERN STUDIES**

# Middle Eastern Capitalism

## NINE ESSAYS

# Middle Eastern Capitalism

## NINE ESSAYS

### A. J. Meyer

**HARVARD UNIVERSITY PRESS**

**Cambridge, Massachusetts**

**1959**

*To the memory of my father*

# Preface

This is a presumptuous little book. In scandalously few pages it tries to illuminate a very complex subject — the Middle East economy. Although it was written for the nonspecialist reader, I hope that an occasional student of the area will learn from its pages.

Economists will most certainly query the absence of indifference curves, analysis based on incremental capital output ratios, capital coefficients. Orientalists will note the book's failure to interpret Middle Eastern economic development as flowing from subtleties translated from Ugaritic potsherd inscriptions. They are quite right.

A word about the title. Capitalism seems still, in 1959, a reasonably accurate description of the Middle East economy. Although governmental expenditures are rising each year, as public-private investment ratios change, the portions of area-wide national incomes spent by governments still average out at about the rate current in the United States. Middle Easterners are, according to experts on the subject, as acquisitively inclined as we capitalist Westerners. Several countries practice extremely conservative monetary policies. Nowhere does socialism seem the word for it — except perhaps in Israel. A mosaic of widely variant "isms," the Middle East today retains much of what we know as capitalism.

The ideas and opinions in these pages have developed during my eight years' residence in the Middle East and subsequent four years' teaching economics and working in the Center for Middle Eastern Studies and the Pakistan Project at Harvard University. My debt to former students at the American University of Beirut and at Harvard — particularly those who have taken Economics 244d — is immense.

At the risk of straining friendships, I have sought criticism from a number of scholars and Middle East experts. The following have read the entire manuscript and given liberally of their advice: Professors H. A. R. Gibb, Alfred Bonné, J. B. Condliffe, Everett Hagen, Charles Issawi, D. W. Lockard, Mr. David Finnie, Mr. and Mrs. Harley Stevens, Mr. Max Thornburg, and Dr. Fakhry Chehab. Shorter parts of the manuscript have been commented on, and improved by, Professors George Kirk, Mohammed Diab, Simon Kuznets, and Richard Robinson, and by Mr. Simos Vassiliou and Mrs. Kathleen Langley. They should not be blamed for the book's shortcomings.

I am also grateful to Professors Edward S. Mason, William L. Langer, and Arthur H. Cole for constant stimulus.

Finally, my wife has helped at every turn. Miss Carolyn Cross and Mrs. Kay Pease made a manuscript from my virtually illegible handwriting, and Mrs. Martha Smith put it into shape for the press.

A. J. MEYER
Cambridge, Massachusetts
1959

# Contents

# Middle Eastern Capitalism

## NINE ESSAYS

# I

## The Middle East Economy
**PROGRESS, PROBLEMS, AND PROSPECTS**

Since World War II the Middle East has put on a spurt of economic growth which is even more revolutionary than the area's political contortions. This fact is usually overlooked by the casual Western visitor. It is also often ignored by the newspaper writer or political propagandist intent on describing contrasts with more developed countries rather than rates of change in the Middle East itself. The broad outlines of that growth can now be stated, as a series of careful studies — some area-wide but most limited to one country — have come off the press.[1] These studies show that Middle Eastern countries have, since 1945, recorded economic growth that is startling by any standards, Western or Asian.

At the top of the list stands one of the world's real economic museum pieces, the Shaikhdom of Kuwait. Before World War II the tiny Persian Gulf kingdom — without fresh water, cultivable topsoil, or any known ingredient for economic growth — served as little but market town and rallying point for desert tribes unwilling to ally themselves either to Wahabi Saudi Arabia or Hashemite Iraq. Its pastoral community and urban dhow builders and traders met in Kuwait town or Ahmadi Port to exchange trinkets, and its economy was distinctly unsophisticated.

Since the war, as the Burgan and Neutral Zone oil fields came into production, Kuwait has come to export a million barrels of oil daily — most of it westward by tanker. The Shaikhdom's income has grown proportionately, from about $50 million in 1950 to about $300 million in 1958. Disregarding earnings from other occupations, Kuwaitis' per capita incomes have grown from about $200 to over $1000 in less than a decade. Investment too has skyrocketed. The singularly unprofligate Shaikh Abdullah el-Salem el-Sabbah has poured hundreds of millions into domestic investment. In 1958, for example, his Development Board expected to invest about $200 million (66 per cent of the national income) at home in schools, drainage, water distillation plants, and the usual social overhead. The additional $100 million was scheduled for addition to the estimated $1 billion he had already invested abroad, chiefly in 2½ per cent United Kingdom treasury securities.

With a per capita income multiplying five times in eight years and investment proceeding at a rate designed to confound economists as well as to press the limits of use to which money can be applied, Kuwait is unique in the world. It has set a pace for economic advance unequaled anywhere, at all levels of its society — from its Eton-blazer-clad schoolboys in air-conditioned schools (most of whom entered this world eight years ago under goathair tents) to its affluent merchants and lesser shaikhs, categorized irreverently by local wits as "Cadillac" shaikhs or "Chevrolet" shaikhs, depending on their place in the pecking order. And while the domestic investment goes on, the shaikhdom is accumulating a vast fund abroad, which in another decade could conceivably yield an annual income of $60 million, $200 per Kuwaiti, from United Kingdom and United States securities.

Next to Kuwait, the most striking growth has been registered by Iraq. Mr. K. G. Fenelon, until 1958 adviser in statistics to the Iraq government, has concluded that the country approximately doubled its net per capita income between 1951 and 1956 — a rate of growth of 20 per cent yearly.[2] In the latter year, Fenelon estimates, Iraq achieved an income of about $103 per capita. Most authorities agree that the advance was attributable about two thirds to soaring oil earnings and one third to expansion of the general economy. Investment in Iraq, meanwhile, has gone on at more than 30 per cent of national income yearly.

Behind the oil-rich nations fall four countries whose rates of growth, while not as startling, are nevertheless impressive. These are Cyprus, Israel, Lebanon, and Syria. Sophisticated indeed when compared to other Middle Eastern countries, all began at fairly high levels of income and moved still higher in recent years.

Cyprus typifies the group. Between 1950 and 1957 the half-million Greek and Turkish residents of Aphrodite's isle approximately doubled, at current prices, their per capita income — from about $200 to $400. A fifty per cent inflation and a 1½ per cent population increase in the interim reduced the net per capita gain in real terms to 4–5 per cent yearly — still a remarkable figure. Cyprus meanwhile has invested a steadily rising percentage of its national income. In recent years 20–25 per cent has been standard.

Israel has performed even more impressively. Between 1950 and 1954 — the years for which most accurate assessments have been made — the Jewish state invested about 24 per cent of its national income and advanced its net per capita income by about 6 per cent yearly. This figure, not in itself startling when compared to rates posted by Israel's neighbors, assumes heroic stature when one relates it to population increase and inflation. In the years under scrutiny Israel underwent massive population increase (in some years as much as 20 per cent) and experienced inflation which in one year alone hit 40 per cent. Despite all this, the 6 per cent yearly figure was maintained — largely by increasing productivity (at more than 6 per cent yearly) and by increasing the flow of foreign aid of various kinds.

Operating under quite different circumstances from those in Cyprus and Israel, Lebanon and Syria have also advanced markedly since World War II. Both have invested at 14–18 per cent of national income and have pushed per capita incomes upward at 6–7 per cent yearly — after allowing for inflation (which was minor in both countries) and after allowance for net population increase. Syria now realizes a net per capita income of about $200 and Lebanon just over $300. Both countries have achieved their advances almost entirely through private investment, have followed conservative monetary policies, and have held inflation to negligible levels.

Below these countries fall the Moslem nations with larger populations. Heading the list is Turkey, which advanced its per capita real income from about $160 to $200 between 1950 and 1956, thus achieving a net increase (after adjustment for population growth at 3 per cent yearly) of about 3 per cent per annum. Turks meanwhile invested at 12–15 per cent yearly, and the past decade has seen an extraordinary expansion of economic activity generally.

Even Egypt has gone upstream since 1951, despite the virtually insurmountable obstacle of population increase. Recent estimates by the Egyptian government and the Bank of Egypt conclude that per capita real income in the Egyptian republic moved from $100 in 1951 to $110 in 1956 — an advance of 1½ per cent yearly. Investment meanwhile has hovered around 10 per cent of national income, and is now (since 1952) weighted heavily on the public side. In the light of the responsibly held view that Egypt's net per capita income underwent decline during the half century prior to 1950, the achievement seems phenomenal.

At the bottom by all recognized standards are Iran, Saudi Arabia, and Jordan. In the first two countries oil earnings, while high, either have gone to too few people or have, until very recently, been spread indiscriminately through the societies into channels discouraging domestic investment. Jordan lives from meager agriculture supplemented by an international dole made necessary by its staggering burden of Palestine refugees. Its per capita income is around $100, with little evidence of advance since World War II. Saudi Arabia, despite its soaring oil earnings, has added little to the living standards of the mass of citizens who roam its deserts. In the absence of really accurate censuses or national income surveys conclusions about Iran are hard to draw. These are easier for Jordan, but are invariably gloomy.

In aggregate, therefore, six Middle Eastern countries (Iraq, Kuwait, Israel, Cyprus, Syria, Lebanon), with populations totaling over 13 million, have registered extremely rapid economic growth in the post–World War II decade. One nation, Turkey, with a population of 23 million, has advanced at what can be called a substantial rate. Egypt, with a population of over 20 million, has in the past seven years just about equaled the rates of net per capita income advance of most Western nations over the last half century. And Iran, Saudi Arabia, and Jordan, with populations totaling between 20 and 30 million, have just about held steady. Compared to the area's past achievements, and alongside rates of growth in South Asia and Africa and Latin America, the accomplishment has been remarkable.

Yet when one looks behind the raw figures of national income and investment — described by a London magazine as "the entrails of a society which economists peer at nervously" — there appears a set of problems of truly Himalayan magnitude. A look at these discloses similarities which cross frontiers from the eastern Mediterranean to Baluchistan.

First comes the crucial query, can oil earnings and capital transfers from other foreign sources continue at levels sufficiently high to sustain Middle Eastern economic growth over the long term? To date the performance has been as follows: just over $1 billion total tax-royalty is currently paid yearly by international oil companies to five Middle Eastern governments — Saudi Arabia, Kuwait, Iraq, Iran, and Qatar — plus about $40 million in pipeline transit fees to Syria, Lebanon, and Jordan; Israel balances its annual trade deficit by gifts from international Jewry, amounting to about $250 million yearly, and by German reparations and United States aid in various forms; Turkey has averaged $250 million yearly for a decade from U.S. military and economic assistance, and in 1958 exceeded its average by more than $100 million; Iran in most years has touched $200 million; capital transfers from abroad to the Cyprus government (mainly British base expenditures and tax-royalty from copper sales) in recent years have exceeded $50 million; capital transfers by overseas Cypriots to relatives on the island average almost $10 million yearly; overseas Lebanese send home as much as $50 million yearly; in the last three years the Soviet Union has supplied (or at least promised) economic and military assistance to Syria and Egypt in the amount of almost $1 billion.

In addition, the Middle East's economic growth has been nurtured in the past decade by a flow of foreign balances accumulated during World War II and in the interim between 1945 and the Korean War. A result of wartime currency controls, shipping problems, and shortages of goods, the balances totaled almost $1.5 billion for Egypt alone.[3] Lebanon and Syria likewise had substantial foreign accounts at war's end, and, like Egypt, partially replenished these by selling cotton at inflated prices in the years 1945–1953. Turkey did the same on a more modest scale. These balances are now largely depleted.

The annual total of transfers described above works out to just over $2 billion yearly — $25 for each of the 80 million people involved, a substantial percentage for an area with per capita incomes averaging between $100 and $150.

But having already drawn heavily upon its international disaster sources, and with domestic incomes still too low to provide funds, the Middle East faces the very real problem of acquiring from abroad, by what might be termed "natural" means, sufficient capital for development. The area's capacity to keep these transfers at a high level in coming years will be of key importance.

Corollary to the above problem is the very real one of maintaining westward-moving oil shipments, and earnings from these, at levels sufficient to keep local development programs moving at a satisfactory pace. Here the countries' cooperation with international oil companies is crucial. Connected are a myriad of other elements of indirect importance: United States import quotas for petroleum products, rates of economic expansion in Europe and the Western Hemisphere and the Far East, with resultant rise in the demand for oil, United States antitrust policy toward the international oil companies, political developments in the area which can either close Suez and the pipelines or keep them open, discoveries of competing oil supplies elsewhere in the world — to mention only a few.[4]

In this context the results of Middle Eastern governments' efforts to move the profit split (currently applicable to crude oil prices only, at Persian Gulf ports) nearer to the gasoline pump in Europe or the Western Hemisphere will also have long-run economic significance. These are admittedly unimportant in the immediate future; neither Saudi Arabia nor Iran, the countries reportedly most interested in the arrangement, has funds available to buy into oil company distribution and refining facilities. But these efforts could be important as determinants of future lease policy. Japanese firms have already tried to break the 50–50 split arrangement. The desperate search by American domestic oil companies for cheap crude oil will probably lead more of them into the Middle East. The ability of oil companies and Middle Eastern governments collectively to forge mutually profitable agreements geared to future conditions will be crucial.

No less crucial will be what evolves from Middle Eastern governments' movement toward a form of Texas Railroad Commission for the Middle East. Still vague and unenunciated, the idea is very much a part of the thinking of many Arab nationalists today. Briefly put, it envisions an area-wide agreement to control production and shipments of petroleum from the Middle East. Obviously unworkable so far, and predicated on the assumption that Europe, and perhaps other markets, will remain the domain of Middle Eastern oil, the subject is under increasing discussion whenever Arab leaders meet.

No less important is the third problem worth mentioning, that of the need to develop the capacity of Middle Eastern governments to spend oil earnings effectively. So far, Iraq and Kuwait have done well, by concentrating on water, schools, transport, communication, and obviously needed social overhead investment. Iran, too, has begun efforts toward this end. Yet priorities vary, magnitudes and directions of necessary investment change constantly, and Kuwait, for example, and possibly Iraq have already approached the point where extraordinary ingenuity is required.

To spend oil moneys more effectively, Middle Eastern governments are turning increasingly to economic planning. As practiced in the Islamic Middle East, planning is still highly conservative. It consists essentially of public investments to harness rivers, save rainfall, shorten the area's vast distances with airlines, roads, and railways, and improve levels of education and public health. But when the limits of this type of investment are reached, urgent decisions must be made on the roles of government and private enterprise as the economic base broadens, industry becomes more important, and requirements in the private sector rise. Even Lebanon and Syria, having hit the end of a ten-year private investment boom, are turning to planning.[5] The wisdom of the economic planners and the response of the mass of citizens to public investments will be of utmost importance.

Another problem facing Middle Eastern nations is competition between funds for economic development and military outlays. While in numerical terms armament expenditures in the Middle East are dwarfed by those of the more "civilized" nations of the world — particularly the United States and the Soviet Union — percentages of national income devoted to defense are uncomfortably high. The area-wide average now approaches ten per cent of national income, a comparable percentage to what we spend in the United States each year. Israel, with a national income of about $1.25 billion, spends over $100 million yearly on defense; Egypt with about $2.5 billion spends over $200 million; Turkey, Syria, Iran, and Iraq strike about the same percentages.

During the past decade some of these expenditures have unquestionably been justified by political circumstances. Maintenance of internal order in Turkey and Iran and prevention of widespread Soviet penetration into Kurdistan and Azerbaijan have resulted in part from military strength in the two countries. The Republic of Syria has realized great economic benefits from expansion of wheat and cotton growing in its northern Jezira province — possible only since 1945 when the Syrian army tamed a hitherto unmanageable Bedouin domain. Israel has consolidated itself in a decade despite implacable opposition from its neighbors on all sides. The Iraq army unquestionably exerts a restraining influence on Kurdish tribesmen in the north. Throughout the area military investments have added in some degree to economic advance.

But the competition between military funds and those for development is now out of hand. In the area under scrutiny almost $750 million is now being invested each year in armaments — roughly the amount necessary to install the sets of necessary social overhead improvements now on the drawing boards yet so far starved for funds. Each expenditure for arms triggers a corresponding "defense" purchase across a nearby frontier. And the West's monopoly (or more correctly, oligopoly) over providing arms to Middle Eastern nations — before 1956 challenged only by Czech arms imports to Israel — has now been broken by the staggering provision of armaments worth over $500 million by Russia to Syria and Egypt in only two years. The tragedy of Western participation in Middle East armament becomes evident when one looks beyond the competition to the fact that in this age of nuclear weapons, jet aircraft, and rockets no Middle Eastern army as now constituted could effectively oppose the Soviet Union — presumably the reason for United States and United Kingdom aid to those armies.

Another problem pertains to the Middle East's terms of trade. The trade-chart curves since 1945 have been jagged — sometimes up, sometimes down, but never completely free of the specter of rising import costs and dropping export prices. For a decade, oil producing countries have enjoyed rising incomes as petroleum prices and production have stayed high. Soaring world copper prices and increased production on Cyprus have benefited the island's economy greatly. High grain and cotton prices during the Korean War were a temporary boon to the economies of Syria, Egypt, and Turkey. There have been, in short, major deterrents to wholesale depreciation of the area's trading position.

Yet the outlook does not permit unbridled optimism. In less than ten years Western technology has substituted rayon and nylon for Egyptian long-staple cotton in the world's automobile tire casings. Dependent on cotton exports to feed herself, Egypt faces monotonously regular market gluts and dropping prices. And Egypt is turning increasingly to the Soviet Union for outlets. Syria and Turkey feel the same pressure. Many Middle Eastern countries — Cyprus, Israel, and Lebanon, for example — can now import wheat more cheaply than they can produce it, yet they have few commodities to sell abroad competitively to earn necessary foreign exchange. All countries in the area face steadily rising import costs for machinery, produced in the West in economies where the wage-push and yearly price inflation have become standard equipment. World copper prices halved between 1955 and 1958, from 50 cents a pound to 25 cents, with resultant lower income to Cyprus. Expansion of demand for petroleum products has likewise fluctuated between 6 per cent and 2 per cent yearly in the United States and between 12 per cent and 9 per cent in Europe, while new oil fields are coming into production in Venezuela and North Africa. The pessimistic proponents of terms-of-trade arguments cannot be dismissed summarily, despite the Middle East's hitherto strong position in this respect.

Still another problem is the area's inability so far to develop really effective interregional trading and capital-flow arrangements. The evidence of this makes a long and dreary story. Kuwait is purportedly the largest single supplier of capital to the London money market, yet nearby Turkey and Iran each year send missions westward seeking funds for development; no really workable inter-Arab trading arrangement has yet been forged, as can be attested by any visitor who has seen the endless queue of trucks which has distinguished the Lebanese-Syrian, Syrian-Iraq, and Syrian-Jordanian frontiers for a decade. Despite endless engineering surveys and countless trips by United States government "trouble shooters," the schemes to harness the Jordan for the use of Israel and her Arab neighbors have come to nothing. Interregional trade within the Middle East totals about 15 per cent of the total, while trade with the West accounts for about 66 per cent; nor, understandably, has there evolved multilateral trade between Jew and Arab. The inter-Arab trade agreement of 1954 has only begun to bring Arab states together as traders. To date political considerations have precluded lasting economic cooperation.

Still another problem concerns the Palestine refugees, resettlement of whom is an essential prelude to any lasting peace and regional economic cooperation in the area. Currently grouped a million strong in camps just outside Israel's frontiers in Gaza, Jordan, Syria, and Lebanon, the refugees stand collectively as the Middle East's "shook-up" generation. The better educated, middle-class professional and merchant families have long since departed, to America and England or to take up citizenship in Lebanon, Syria, Iraq, or Jordan. Those left are mainly former peasants possessed of few skills or trades. Living on an international dole of $2 per person monthly, they are pathetic indeed, and their sole visible accomplishment is to procreate themselves by 3 per cent per year.

Economic resettlement of the refugees awaits a decision by Iraq, and to a lesser extent Syria, to accept them as immigrants. (Jordan has already doubled its population with refugees, and Egypt can hardly add further to its population.) Once this step is taken the capital requirements for resettlement must be met. Estimated conservatively at $500 per person (Israel assumes it must invest about $2500 per Jewish immigrant), the total bill becomes at least $500 million — about twice the West's total investment in feeding the refugees since 1948.[6] So far, neither the will to resettle the hapless souls nor the capital to permit it seems forthcoming from any quarter. The Arabs remain obstinate. And Israel regularly issues proposals for resettlement which are at once well intentioned and irrelevant.

The refugees, meanwhile, have played a distinct role in the Middle East's recent economic expansion. Flight capital brought from Palestine (or transferred from British Banks after 1948) by refugees accounted for much of the building boom in Beirut, Amman, and Damascus. Middle-class Palestinians have proved highly creative as industrial and commercial entrepreneurs. And camp-dwellers have afforded a source of low-wage labor which some observers feel has stimulated industrialization by the usual process of permitting high entrepreneurial profits and rates of reinvestment.

Another problem concerns the effect on Middle Eastern nations of the intensified Soviet economic offensive. Since 1955 directed chiefly at Syria and Egypt, the effort has gained momentum yearly. Except for arms imports (which by 1958 came to exceed an estimated $500 million), the commodity composition of Middle East trade has remained unaltered. But directions *have* changed, particularly for "problem" commodities such as Egyptian cotton. And a steady increase of exports is under way from Syria and Egypt to Communist-bloc countries. In 1951, for example,

9 per cent of Egypt's exports went to Soviet-dominated areas. In mid-1959 more than 50 per cent of her exports (mostly cotton) went there. Imports from the same areas have risen from 6 per cent to 14 per cent over the same period.[7]

Russia has supplemented her trade offensive with low-cost development loans — 2½ per cent in most instances, repayable over 12 to 20 years, largely with Middle Eastern commodities. Enunciated in a series of agreements remarkable for their lack of visible conditions, these were clearly designed for reproduction in local newspapers and to portray the essentially benign nature of the Russian signatory. In Syria the loans pay capital costs for, and provide technicians to, a series of water, drainage, and communications projects. The Russians have not hesitated to help on schemes originally suggested to the Syrian government by Western advisers working with the International Bank or private consultant firms. Commitments for economic and technical assistance total about $300 million.[8]

The new Russian effort has likewise been distinguished by its break of the West's monopoly over military shipments to the area. Since the Czech arms deal with Israel of 1948, America, France, and Britain have provided virtually all the military hardware and defense support funds not only to Israel but to the Arab states and Turkey and Iran as well. Syria and Egypt's economic pacts with the Soviet Union have been accompanied by military assistance arrangements valued at more than $500 million since 1956. Like Western nations, Russia seems to be weighting her Middle East investments at about two dollars of military funds for one dollar of economic aid.

To date the relationship has had ambiguous results. Inexperienced as traders, some Soviet-bloc countries have been unable to produce the export commodities, mostly machinery, promised for delivery under aid contracts. Nor have Russian armaments proved universally superior to Western arms.[9] Substantial quantities of Egyptian cotton, sent to Russia, have found their way to Lancashire via Finland at prices cheaper than British spinners paid earlier to their regular Egyptian suppliers. The sword has proved distinctly double-edged, and results so far have sobered an occasional thinking citizen.

The next problem concerns the snail-like shift in the structure of the economies of most Middle Eastern nations. Countries of the world which have in the past sustained rapid growth have done so by constantly adding machinery to the productive process, through industrialization. The resultant increase in the ratio of hands working to mouths eating has accounted for the great periods of growth over time. A drop in rural and a rise in urban population has accompanied the process. The United States and Britain typify the trend.

But to date the Middle East reveals no sharp shift in economic structure. Despite the burgeoning cities, there is little evidence that rural-urban population ratios have changed substantially since 1950. Nor has industry anywhere (except in Israel) begun to challenge agriculture as a major employer.[10] The area-wide occupation breakdown still, as it has for a quarter century, finds more than half the breadwinners in agriculture and less than 10 per cent in industry, yet these occupations together produce only about the same portion of the national income as the trade sector. (Israel, with its conscious effort to keep its citizens on the soil, defies comparison in this context.)

Finally, and no list of problems can ignore it, must be mentioned the upsurge of population pressure. Israel has tripled her population in a decade, mostly through immigration but with some assistance from natural increase. Egypt at its present rate of climb stands to double her populace each twenty years. The area-wide rate of increase is between

2 and 3 per cent yearly, and evidence exists to permit the conclusion that not only Israel and Egypt but also Turkey, Syria, Iraq, and the Palestine refugees might well be exceeding 3 per cent. Each year, in short, the area under scrutiny assumes an added burden of 2.5 million new citizens to feed, clothe, and provide with the customary amenities. Only Lebanon and Cyprus seem capable of keeping their increase at less than 2 per cent, and this they do by emigration.

So much for the problems. To relate the past decade's economic performance to these obstacles and forecast the Middle East's capacity to overcome them is hazardous indeed. Nevertheless, now that we know more about the area's economies, some tentative conclusions about future prospects may be drawn.

First, the economic performance at the public level of countries such as Israel and Iraq and of private investors in Syria, Lebanon, and Turkey has shown remarkable vitality and leads one to the conclusion that in these countries at least the human capacities are present for sustained advance. If investment can continue, if international trade and capital flows stay high, if demand continues to rise as it has recently — to mention only a few of the conditions — chances seem distinctly bright.

Next, we have now seen enough to conclude that America's extremely successful experience with ECA in Europe — in which economic aid produced truly miraculous results — has relatively little meaning for the non-Western, cereal- and rice-eating peoples who inhabit the villages of the Islamic Middle East. So different are the resource patterns, histories, structures of economies, capacities to govern, and breeds of man, that projections based on postwar Europe's response to transfusions of public capital become virtually meaningless.

Third, we now know that a temporal safety margin still

exists for most of the Middle East. In raw terms of man-land ratios and capital available for investment, the sixty million people of Turkey, Iran, Israel, and the northern Arab countries (Egypt, unfortunately, must be excluded from the generalization) still have time to install more productive plants, slow down population growth, and change ratios of hands working to mouths eating. The hopeless imbalance in these respects which distinguishes most of Asia today has not really hit the Middle East. To measure the safety margin is, of course, impossible. But it might, hopefully, be as long as a generation.

Fourth, and in this same context, we now know enough about the Middle East economies to conclude that the paucity of resources still puts very definite limits on long-term growth. Until and unless major breakthroughs in technology occur, the area faces very definite ceilings above which it cannot go. Like the safety margin above, this ceiling defies exact measurement. To hope, for example, for per capita incomes much above $500 yearly (roughly a quarter that of the United States in 1958) for most of the Middle East would be to strain the limits of optimism. But even this would be a dramatic improvement.

Finally, despite predictions of optimistic economists, who describe takeoffs into sustained growth after periods of foreign aid, or of the equally emphatic Cassandras who see the Western world inevitably getting richer while Asia and the Middle East get poorer, we really don't know what will happen. The Western world's economic history permits thought-provoking analogies, but it has so far failed to provide policies guaranteed to succeed. And the mountain of recent literature has proved little but that economists and other observers are themselves more than confused on the subject.

# II

## Historical Analogies and Middle East Economic Development

Comparison between areas of the world at similar — or rather, what seem to be similar — stages of history is a provocative and intriguing task. It is also highly treacherous. People differ, as do nations, and the historian seeking explanation for the modern Middle East in mercantilist Europe, for example, needs a thick skin, unassailable reputation, or, better yet, a combination of the two. A Toynbee can try it, but most others choose safer ground, where the footnotes bear more authority and derision from one's colleagues is less fatal.

Oddly enough, economists, usually a more conservative breed, have until very recently also accepted tacitly Toynbee's belief that economic development is sufficiently analogous so that the theories used to explain and forecast economic change in the West are relevant to a developing East. In writing about development economics, their concern has been largely with factor proportions, quantitative measurements, and the inevitable accompaniment, money and its role in influencing directions and magnitudes of growth. All admit publicly the differing societal infrastructure, widely variant levels of technology, and so on. But so far most have skirted the questions raised by pre-Keynesian institutional economists and have directed their attention to capital output ratios, allowable limits of inflationary finance, foreign aid levels, and the rest. A Toynbee-like assumption of historical relativity has, with few exceptions, punctuated the thinking of Western economists concerned with economic development.

Lately, however, the number of exceptions to the above rule has grown. Some, such as Professor Gottfried Haberler, have launched frontal assaults on the acceptance abroad of the validity of a series of sacred Western economic concepts.[1] Others, less hostile to historical and theoretical relativity, but nevertheless uncomfortable about the uses to which Western economic theory is being put, have begun re-exploration of the relevance of Western history to Asian economic development — employing not only Western historical data but, more important, experience gained recently in a changing East. Edward Mason, Everett Hagen, and Kenneth Galbraith typify this view. Their writings reflect increasingly an effort to find meaningful analogies, to reject those theoretical concepts of dubious value — for example the widely held view that Eastern economic development might best copy the West's ratios of public to private investment — and to shape new ones for a region building its economic structure almost entirely on a base of imported technology.[2] They are increasingly preoccupied with the "preconditions" for economic growth, and with the periods — the nineteenth century and earlier — which bear relevance.

With the argument yet unsettled, and probably due to remain so for some time, the Western scholar and thoughtful layman can add much to his understanding of Middle Eastern economic development by placing several of the elements of that phenomenon alongside a reasonable counterpart in Western history. For Middle Easterners seeking markers above the shoals and depths to chart courses for their new nations, the process is equally illuminating. What follows suggests that mercantilist Europe, with its combination of governments intent on promoting economic development and populations essentially innocent of "preconditional" experience, offers as fruitful analogies with the modern Middle East as do later periods of history — particularly the often-chosen nineteenth century.

One such analogy may be found in the interplay between the two great opposites of the early modern era — sixteenth-century Spain, and England under the Tudor and Stuart monarchs. Faced with a not dissimilar challenge, the import of an incredible quantity of capital, bullion and coined gold and silver, Spain for a century reacted one way, and emerged bankrupt. Britain reacted in another and set the stage for affluence.

Put briefly, the sixteenth-century spice-trading merchants and Mesta landowners who shaped public policy in Ferdinand and Isabella's kingdom proved thoroughly incapable of working into their nation's economic life the two hundred tons of gold and eighteen thousand tons of silver dug by the Conquistadors in Mexico and Peru. Rather than factories, jobs for more people, and a reforming agriculture, Spain's legacy was price inflation, case-hardening of an already rigid class structure, and perpetuation of an apathetic peasantry. When her glorious hundred years of Western Hemisphere conquest and bullion transfer were finished, Spain declined quickly to what has proved an enduring national unimportance and economic torpor. She proved that money alone was not enough.

Britain reacted differently to the challenge of capital from the New World. Her government and merchants and landowners, like those in Holland, stood ready to turn Spain's price inflation to their own use. Their manufactured goods, banking services, shipping companies, piracy, and general capacity for enterprise made Spain but a temporary stopping point for New World gold and silver. The multiplier churned in England, drawing Spain's wealth northward to strengthen sterling, trigger investment throughout the British economy, and help create the first really competent blend of capitalism and nationalism in the Western World.

Some Arab states to date have exhibited this same trend toward what Benjamin Higgins has, in other contexts, termed "dualistic economies." [3] Saudi Arabia serves as a modern counterpart of sixteenth-century Spain. Oil royalties have grown since World War II to exceed $300 million yearly, and the desert kingdom has received capital transfers — much of it in gold — from the West exceeding $2 billion over the past decade. With consummate efficiency, the Saudi ruling families joined with the peninsula's tribal Bedouin tradition to bury the gold in the ground, to hang it on the nation's women, or to convert it into foreign-made consumers' goods. Skilled practitioners of the world-wide art of conspicuous consumption, Saudis have with few exceptions — chiefly the magnificent set of government ministries in Riyadh, ports in Jeddah and Dammam, and an inadequate set of schools and hospitals — spent their money with (by standards of the Protestant Christian West) extraordinary profligacy.

Except for the last two years (when investments in small industries servicing the oil camps in the Eastern Province of Al Hasa have touched $10 million yearly) Saudi shaikhs and entrepreneurs have preferred to invest abroad what surpluses they had, some in Western corporate securities and some in apartment houses in Beirut, Cairo, and Damascus. The gold has come and gone and little has taken hold creatively. Preconditions for sustained growth have clearly not been met.

Nearby Iraq and Lebanon, sister Arab states, more nearly parallel Britain in the analogy. Better educated, longer in contact with the West, having governments more responsible and responsive to popular needs than Saudi Arabia's, these countries have gained substantially from Middle East capital inflows. Lebanon's entrepreneurs have swarmed to the oil countries — building bridges and pipelines, operating truck fleets and airlines, importing goods, on occasion beginning their manufacture in Beirut, processing fresh fruits and vegetables for sale in the Persian Gulf. Like Britain in 1580, Lebanon today is an efficient capital sponge, drawing oil royalties back westward in return for its services and also into investment in apartment houses and land in its (prior to the summer of 1958) stable economic environment. While maintaining strong currency and stable prices at home, Lebanese have profited from inflation and economic instability elsewhere, particularly in the Persian Gulf kingdoms and shaikhdoms. Lebanon's record of growth, largely attributable to private investments, has proved astounding.

Iraq, too, has grown mightily, doubling its national income in the past five years. Yet its pattern varies greatly from Lebanon's. Investments in water and drainage, soil improvement, transport and communications, low-cost housing, have all been under public authority. In recent years Iraq has invested more than $200 million yearly, $40 per citizen, in social overhead improvements. But direction has come entirely from the top, via a ruling elite, and Iraq's response to capital inflows has not yet galvanized, as in Lebanon, the entire citizenry to acquisitive endeavor. Iraq lies between Lebanon and Saudi Arabia in its response to the tinkle of gold sovereigns and Turkish rashadis.

Another analogy pertains to trade, or rather the lack of it, between the Arab states and Israel today. The casual observer understandably views the increased tightening of the Arab boycott as essentially negative — a throttle on a relationship which might, through exchange of goods and services, lead to political understanding. In this instance, American economic history offers a comparable example.

I refer to the trading relationship between the northern and southern United States in the decades after the Civil War. In these years an industrializing North, using its own (and British) capital, underwent extraordinary economic expansion. Resting on a base of yeoman agriculture, moving toward the 160-acre ideal of a later period, factories and trades burgeoned in the Middle West, Eastern Seaboard, and New England. Lack of restricting traditions, cheap labor, copious entrepreneurial drive and skill, and the safety value of new Western lands kept the Northern economy on a steadily upward, if occasionally irregular, path.

The South, on the other hand, changed slowly. Its shift from the pre–Civil War slave-owning and plantation base to a monoproductive, sharecropping cotton and tobacco economy was gradual indeed. Until as late as 1930, the American South rated as a definitely undeveloped area. The South's real momentum of economic growth and expansion has been a phenomenon of the 1940's and 1950's.

Trade between North and South after the Civil War can hardly be labeled a promoter of harmony between peoples, nor did it lead, through its internal mercantilism, to amelioration of the economic plight of the South. For almost a century the South stoked Northern factories with wood pulp, cotton, tobacco, and leather, while serving as an outlet (first via the packsacks of carpetbaggers, later through mail-order houses) for cheaper manufactured goods from the North. Yet the apocryphal story of the "poor white" farmer wearing clothes made from Southern cotton but manufactured in the North, lighting a cigarette also made in the North from Southern tobacco and paper pulp, with a match created by the same process, while he went barefoot, was uncomfortably true.

This same lack of harmony between economic institutions permeates the relationship between Israel and her Arab neighbors today. Israel needs many of the raw materials currently produced in nearby Arab countries — cotton for her textile mills, cottonseed meal for her fishponds, food grains for her bakeries, oil for her industry and motor transport. Today she buys most of these in the world's most expensive markets, while the world's cheapest sources lie tantalizingly near to her frontiers. Likewise nearby and also denied to her is a rich market outlet for cheap manufactured goods, now being serviced by United States, German, and British suppliers. The hermetic seal undeniably helps keep Israel's trade deficit high.

Yet if the North-South analogy bears relevance, the Arab economic boycott conceivably has elements to recommend it, to Arabs and Israelis. Israel, with an economy shored up by $250 million yearly in gifts and loans from abroad, obviously could do well with cheaper raw materials and broadened market outlets. As throughout her economy, decisions on pricing and other considerations could be made with only partial reference to economic profitability. Although few Israelis might favor it, the trading relationship at this juncture could probably only lead to promotion of the different economies furthered by post–Civil War North-South trade in the United States.

The key to a successful trading relationship obviously lies in institutional change on both sides of the Arab-Israeli frontiers, but more particularly on the Arab side. Until the basic structure of the Arab economies changes — with more industry, altered ratios of rural-urban wage earners, increased productivity all around, Arab countries would be easy prey for Israeli economic penetration of an exploitive sort. On these terms the Israelis' much discussed (and probably sincerely believed in) "mission" to the underdeveloped Middle East can only attract in the Arab countries an audience comparable in enthusiasm with the Southern United States upon hearing Northern exhortations on the same subject — even prior to Little Rock! And trade would not promote the mutually advantageous development through natural selection found so frequently in Western history. Once the Arab states industrialize, and political confidence grows on both sides of the frontiers, trade might help rather than exacerbate an already unpleasant relationship.

A third analogy is the role played by grassland farming in the evolution of the world's most developed countries and in the Middle East today. The topsoil of northern Europe, the United Kingdom, and North America — intensively farmed but, in recent years at least, carefully, almost tenderly, preserved — has relied heavily on nitrogen-fixing hay crops for sustenance. Rotation of cereal grains and grasses and industrial crops such as sugar beets and cotton has played a central role in the expanding Western agricultural economy. Today 75 per cent of the topsoil of England and America is devoted to grasses at some stage of the crop cycle. In the West the blade of grass has been central to diversified farming, making possible increased output of cereal grains and animal protein foods (meat, dairy products) from the same acreage.

Western diets have responded. Today most citizens of "developed" countries eat meals heavily weighted toward meat, dairy products, and other animal fats, with cereals occuying only about twenty-five per cent of total intake. The combination of consumer response and change in agricultural production has influenced the whole fabric of

Western society — industrial growth based on farm products, size of farms, life expectancy due to improved diet,
even the leading cause of death increasingly identified as
heart disease stemming from cholesterol-clogged arteries
caused by diets too high in animal fats.

Relating hay to history, V. G. Simkhovich has suggested that the lack of grasses on the hillsides of Greece
and Rome contributed to the decline of those ancient civi-
lizations.[4] Briefly put, Simkhovich's argument holds that
dropping yields of wheat and barley on a soil unreplenished
by root crops or adequate fertilizers upset the entire balance
of both the internal and international economies of the
Mediterranean cultures. In time, soil depletion helped de-
stroy the yeoman farmers and drove them to the cities or to
the latifundia, forced expansion of terrace agriculture devoted to grapes and olive production, and in so doing contributed to Greek and Roman expansion abroad in search
of bread grains — to be acquired by military conquest or
in exchange for vats of wine and olive oil. Hay growing,
Simkhovich implies, might have braked the downhill movement of the ancient economies and set them on a quite different course.

Without laboring the analogy, it is safe to conclude that
in its soil depletion most of the Middle East today resembles
latter-day Greece and Rome. Yet with three centuries of
Western soil chemistry, petrochemical development, and
agricultural improvement to draw on, the area at last has
a chance to improve its mined topsoil and broaden its rural
base. Israel and Turkey have already launched grassland
farming efforts, experiments in animal crop agriculture, and
systematic campaigns to increase output of protein crops.
In an area short of water, whose ecology has been radically
altered by the parasitic behavior of man (and goat), these
will take time, and results are only partially visible. The

occasional hay-baler (a symbol of dynamic agriculture in the West) which one encounters in Anatolia or on the west bank of the Jordan, or the neatly packaged cheeses and graded meats in Tel Aviv and Ankara, mark a definite start.

The role that grassland farming can play in the Middle East today admittedly depends in large part on two elements: first, the extent to which modern plant-breeding can evolve root crops suitable to eastern Mediterranean soils and low rainfall, and the willingness of the Middle Eastern rural mind to adopt them; and second, the speed with which grassland agriculture can be given widespread introduction. Put in other terms, an acre of land devoted to cereals produces seven times more calories than an acre of land grazing animals or producing animal feed. In an area near starvation after reaching the point of overpopulation, the shift away from wheat and rice growing to mixed farming becomes almost impossible — as in the Far East today. The Middle East still, in man-land terms, has a slight safety margin. And grass takes shape as a crucial element in the process of economic development.

The fourth analogy of merit pertains to the similarity between the effects on trade of the fifteenth century Ottoman conquest of the Middle East and what Charles Issawi has recently termed the "emerging Arab monopoly of Eastern Mediterranean trade routes." [5] Historical revisionism has consistently rejected Moslem-Christian conflict as explanation for the European traders' abandoning the overland roads after 1480 and has explained the shift to the Cape route in terms of excessive cargo losses (from brigandage resulting from lack of public order) and the cupidity of Mamluk and Ottoman merchants and tax collectors. Financial and political, not religious, reasons were doubtless the main elements diverting eastern Mediterranean trade after 1500.

Today political developments within and among the Arab states point toward the evolution of a similar situation. Internal politics and anti-Western sentiment in the Arab East have already led to temporary severance of the East-West trade arteries — the Suez Canal and the oil pipeline from Iraq to the Mediterranean. As the move from Arab political unity progresses, chances seem good that the pressure will grow, not only with regard to pipelines and ship passage but conceivably toward coordinated demands for revision of tax-royalty agreements between Western oil companies and Middle Eastern governments.

In coping with these demands for greater income from local governments, Western oil companies and governments will do well to remember that despite the troubles after 1460, a brisk trade continued between Europe and the Levant, that the urban communities throughout the Middle East have roots deep in the capitalist tradition, and that it is in the interest of all concerned that amicable change in agreements be made as changing circumstances warrant. In this respect, Western oil companies, originators of the fifty-fifty profit-split arrangement, have already proved most sophisticated.

Yet Arab governments must exhibit similar sophistication if mutually satisfactory arrangements are to ensue. Orderly marketing of the daily four million barrels of westward-moving oil requires sizable restraint on the part of producing governments. To keep market outlets open, refineries and tanker fleets operative, companies must earn satisfactory profits. Glutted markets for petroleum products in 1958 have proved, among other things, that the international oil companies, despite their efficient marketing arrangements in Europe and the Western Hemisphere, face formidable problems and badly need a cooperative attitude from oil supplying countries.

Further influencing the whole relationship today is the same onrush of technology which exhibited itself so vividly in Ottoman times. Indeed the relationship has definitely proved a breeder of technology. Added risks and expense on shipments to the East via Constantinople and Alexandria undeniably triggered the application by fifteenth century Portuguese and Spanish shipowners of knowledge (known earlier but never really applied) of navigation, ship-design, and other elements of marine technology. These made possible the use of the Cape route to India. The closing of the Suez Canal in 1956 created another upsurge in marine technology through perfections in design and construction of the 100,000-ton super oil tanker — powered by nuclear engines and able to move Persian Gulf oil to Europe via South Africa at costs approximating the Suez route for conventional vessels. (Oddly enough, the opening of Suez in the mid-nineteenth century is credited with forcing the application of steam power to vessel propulsion.)

Pipeline technology has also responded to the Middle East's challenge with a myriad of construction and pumping improvements. Lines designed to by-pass troubled political areas (for example, the recently discussed pipeline from northern Iran to the eastern Mediterranean via southern Turkey) are now technically feasible — despite the Middle East's high mountains and extremes of climate and distance. The existence of Israel, astride the land barrier between the Gulf of Aqaba and the Eastern Mediterranean and anxious to apply Western technology — pipelines and the rest — to advance itself, also rates as a technological element in the relations between the West and the emerging Arab monopoly of direct trade routes.

The final analogy meriting speculation is one comparing the myriad decrees of the mercantilist monarchs of sixteenth and seventeenth century Europe with economic de-

velopment plans in the Middle East today. The processes
have striking elements of similarity.

The Tudor and Stuart monarchs in England and continental rulers such as Louis XIV, while undeniably interested in cementing the controls of an absolute royalty, were
constantly preoccupied with economic advance. Their decrees, numbering in the thousands and ubiquitously present
in the national life of the period, dealt with everything,
from export rulings, to weights and measures, to land enclosure. Throughout the policy ran a central, if admittedly
unstated, theme: increased gross national product through
reallocation of resources and income by fiat. Termed "state
making on the economic side" by one historian, mercantilism in many ways parallels economic planning in the
modern Middle East.[6]

Middle East development plans run the gamut of govern-
ment-promoted economic growth. Some call for the state
or quasi-public bodies to operate as well as begin new
ventures. Others see the state as most useful in expanding,
rather than beginning, undertakings launched by private
enterprise. Some limit themselves to social-overhead investments. All increasingly tend toward land reform of varying
degrees of severity — modern counterparts of the enclosure movement.

Although the plans are run by republican governments
and military juntas rather than by kings, the measures they
promulgate are rapidly permeating the entire fabric of
Middle Eastern society. Comparison between them and
mercantilist decrees leads to the following conclusions:
first, the process is snowballing and seems bound to continue unless a miraculous upswing in private investment
somehow develops; second, as was true, as Eli Heckscher
has made clear, of the mercantilist decrees in Sweden,
nobody really knows what the results will be;[7] and third,

in view of the societal preconditions facing both sixteenth century Europe and the Middle East today, comparing the onslaught of forced-draft economic growth on these two societies may well prove more meaningful than analogies drawn from later periods of history.

# III

## *Reflections on Entrepreneurship*

Those trying to understand economic development in the Middle East face intricate problems when they try to relate the businessman and his actions to the process.[1] Which comes first, a phalanx of enterprisers making their own opportunities and demand for each other's products, or investments and regulations by the state which postulate and set the stage for the private entrepreneur?

Defenders of the first position draw their support, consciously or unconsciously, from nineteenth century classical economics and Joseph Schumpeter. To them the entrepreneur is all-important. It is he who must appear and, double-entry bookkeeping pad in hand, charge through the economic frontier engaging in what Schumpeter euphemistically termed "creative destruction." The process obviously has its disagreeable aspects, in the shape of a certain amount of exploitation of labor, imperfect competition pushed as far as the monopolist can manage it, and so on. But net results are on the whole good. Inevitably Say's law that "what sells one good is the production of another" is borne out as the enterprisers create goods, purchasing power for each other's goods, and city jobs for underemployed rural villagers. Cumulatively the process destroys the vicious circle of low purchasing power inhibiting increased output that was enunciated so graphically by Professor Ragnar Nurkse in his Cairo lectures.[2]

Adherents of this view accept the need for public investment in the usual "social overhead" ventures — highways, communications, and public-health medicine. But these are not regarded as the basic determinants of economic destiny. The entrepreneur is still the catalyst, and the aggregate of his capacities sets the course for economic development.

When thinking about the Middle East, a substantial number of Western economists adopt this approach. Aligned with them are most Western businessmen with Middle East interests, including oilmen, and many representatives of United States and other non-Communist governments resident in the area. Supporters of the view cross liberal and conservative political party lines.

So too do the environmentalists, who, in opposition, hold that the peculiar amalgam of resources, human attitudes, and historical background in the Middle East today makes necessary centralized planning efforts which will utilize the profit-seeking entrepreneur much less than did the capitalist West. Eventually the enterpriser will have his chance. But for now the major investment decisions will be made by the state, the military entrepreneur, or, as in Israel, by quasi-public bodies such as the Histadrut. Skilled managers and decision makers will be necessary and useful, but the entrepreneur of the eighteenth and nineteenth century American and British model will be at best a junior partner.

The environmentalists without doubt enjoy majority status in this Middle Eastern version of the wrangle over the priority of the chicken or the egg. Middle class civil servants from the eastern Mediterranean to Pakistan, aided by foreign advisers of like persuasion, have enunciated development plans which outline forced-draft economic growth through a series of five- and seven-year plans. The standard ratio of investment current in Israel, Iraq, Iran, and Pakistan, for example, is about 80 per cent public, 20 per cent private — almost the exact opposite of the pre-1930 Western world. For the most part, the planners are extremely conservative people, more than a few of whom see their efforts as essential parts of a vast salvage operation for the capitalist system in a developing East.

Despite their many disagreements, the opponents concur on the need, in all Middle Eastern countries, for intelligent investment decisions, public and private, and for men able to make reasonably sound choices. The entrepreneur, therefore, is still of utmost importance — whether he be a Histadrut official deciding between an investment in a cement factory or a textile mill, a member of the Iraq Development Board allocating expenditure to a drainage project rather than port improvement, a Syrian textile operator buying land with his profits rather than reinvesting them in his factory, or a Lebanese businessman deciding whether or not to buy a planeload of gold bullion in transit to Saudi Arabia. The wellsprings of investment decisions are of utmost importance to economic development in the Middle East. So too are the men making the decisions.

In most countries of the Islamic Middle East, commercial capitalism is still the dominant system. Although most people still live from agriculture, inordinately high proportions of national incomes still arise from commercial sources or allied financial ventures. In the last decade industry has acquired some importance in national income accounts, but overseas trade, import-export, transportation, and merchant banking are still the large money earners and the most efficient enterprises.

The efficiency, of course, is relative. Except in a few firms, the rational business practices of the West are absent. Operating without great inventories, large payrolls, or customer credit, the Levantine businessman has scant need for the business machinery and accounting practices of the industrial West. And puzzlement besets the American or British businessman visiting the office of a Middle Eastern merchant whom he knows to be a big operator — only to find the latter's headquarters paraphernalia consisting solely of an empty desk, a telephone, a pad of cable blanks, and the merchant's not-too-bright cousin waiting obsequiously for the inevitable order to bring cups of coffee or glasses of Coca-Cola. In this respect Max Weber's definition of a rational capitalist establishment would still exclude most firms in the Islamic Middle East.[3]

The area's history partially explains the situation. From the time of the Roman Empire to the British Raj, Middle Eastern merchants have learned that visible records encouraged tax gathering and that the place to stow one's secrets was in one's retentive memory. Such conditioning is only slowly abandoned.

Yet under proper stimulus the Middle Eastern merchant has shown a willingness to discuss his operations with candor. Contrary to many expectations, for example, the Harvard Business School group in Turkey (cooperating with the University of Istanbul) has found Turkish merchants eager to provide data for the "case-study" teaching technique — data which have, through cross-checking, been proved to be extraordinarily frank and complete. Where he can see a chance for gain (in this instance perhaps mistakenly), the merchant can shed the picturesque deviousness usually attributed to him.

In the merchant's showroom one encounters another situation typical of the era of commercial capitalism in Europe, little specialization into retail and wholesale business, and similarly scant concentration on one brand or type of product.[4] Alongside the exhibited automobile are cases of Scotch whiskey, cartons of "Nuit de Noel," phonograph records, and electric appliances. The situation invariably leads to time-consuming bargaining at all levels, including retail sale. It also encourages the nonimporting retailer to keep changing his line of products. Under such conditions lasting confidence between supplier and retailer, or retailer and consumer, becomes virtually impossible. And the seller seldom really knows his product.

Attendant upon such market organization is the practice of pooling of resources by several firms for a single transaction. Common to Renaissance Italy and mercantilist Britain, these arrangements pertain widely in the Middle East today, for transactions ranging from purchase of a shipload of flour en route from Canada to Suez to acquiring ownership of a consignment of cloth in the free zone in Naples. These alliances form and dissolve with breathtaking speed, and the goods frequently never touch the owners' home port.

Understandably, such operations impart a distinctly international outlook to the commercial communities in Alexandria, Beirut, Teheran, and Karachi and doubtless affect individual political loyalties. The businessman who buys in London or New York and sells in Singapore or Chittagong frequently is more concerned with political and economic developments in these communities than in his own "bedroom" city. And the resultant "commuter mentality" — comparable to that attributed by sociologists to America's suburban commuter businessmen — frequently manifests itself in tax evasion, unwillingness to permit one's sons to do military service, and the other features of a society with divided loyalties.

Another feature of the Middle Eastern outlook which doubtless influences choice of occupation, particularly in the Levant, is the view that the good man in society is not the leader but the "mediator." In economic life the attitude expresses itself in the middleman mentality so prevalent in business in the Arab East today. And the observant Westerner in Beirut is constantly impressed with the esteem society accords the commission agent who amasses a fortune largely through letting his instinct for the "main chance" dictate investment rather than through sustained effort at establishing and running a factory.

Contrary to general opinion, acquisition is, in fact, generally revered. Not by the wildest stretch of imagination could the commercial communities of any Middle Eastern city be labeled as "spiritually oriented" or as holdouts from the chase after mammon. Indeed, to employ Fritz Redlich's phrase, they are every bit as "daimonic" and as much tacit believers in social Darwinism as American and British businessmen of an earlier era.[5] Yet with all the rapacity, there is a basic element of honesty and straightforwardness. Everyone knows where everyone else stands, and it would be unthinkable to disguise larcenous intent with a veil of professional ethics or concern for society at large. The attitude is singularly devoid of hypocrisy and "soul." (In some ways it is refreshing to, and best understood by, any American who has purchased an automobile since World War II. He has often found the transaction distinguished by packed prices, unwanted extra equipment, and car dealer protestations of civic responsibility.) "Soulful" behavior as currently practiced by America's larger corporate directorates is likewise unknown.[6]

Assessment of the origins of industrial entrepreneurship in the Middle East is more difficult. Without question many industrial establishments of the past three decades arose from the standard Middle Eastern stimulant, international disaster in its various forms. In the 1920's, for example, Turkish pressure on the Armenians flooded the Arab countries and Cyprus with men of "producing" mentalities. Later, in the 1930's, troubles in Central Europe and the

business depression in the West combined to encourage
movement to the area of many persons with industrial back-
grounds — Jews, Arabs from South and Central America,
Europeans of various nationalities. World War II led to
more of the same, as Allied armies built up Middle Eastern
purchasing power while hostilities created shortages of
goods. The Arab-Israeli War shifted industry-inclined
Palestinian Arabs to Lebanon, Syria, Iraq, and Jordan, and
more European Jews came to newly created Israel. Soaring
wheat and cotton prices during the Korean War, coupled
with the usual shortages, gave these men a chance to practice their skills. Since 1920, disaster has been a major creator
of a climate for industry in the Middle East.

The displaced Armenians, Jews, European and Arab
refugees, products of international disaster, have played
crucial roles, and they give weight to Schumpeter's arguments about the role of the "creative minority" in economic development. The Palestine Arab refugee is typical.
During the past decade these stateless and second-class
citizens have established models of enterprise in the Levant
far more sophisticated than earlier establishments. The best
garage and machine shop (by Western standards) in Beirut
is run by Palestinians. Locally financed and managed cas-
ualty and life insurance has been largely a creation of a
Palestinian group. Perhaps the most aggressive banking and
industrial combine yet to operate in the Arab East is completely owned and managed by Christian and Moslem
Palestinians.

But the Jew, Armenian, or refugee Arab is not solely
responsible for creative entrepreneurship. Countries such
as Iraq and Turkey have witnessed, particularly during the
past decade, a modest development of home industry by
no means solely attributable to "outsiders." In Aegean
Turkey, for example, where a quarter of the country's in-

dustry is located, industrialists are virtually all Moslem Turks, most of whom were originally traders or came from trading families, few from agriculture. The same applies to Iraq.[7]

In Iran, the situation was similar until a decade or so ago. Since 1945, however, according to recent research on the subject, substantial industrial activity has been going on under the ownership and management of families which for generations were chiefly landowners. The shift has been made without the connecting link of commerce and partially, at least, because of fear of the consequences of the Western impact on Iran. Put simply, Iranian landlords feel that the 1954 oil consortium agreement (which calls for large quantities of local purchasing), the seven-year plan, and American advisers' urging the Shah toward land reform and efficient tax collection signal the end of the old era. They are shifting to industry to avoid disaster.[8]

An outstanding characteristic of the entrepreneurial pattern in the Islamic Middle East is the persistence of the family firm. Most business is still done by family firms, industrial or commercial, and the "destruction of the protecting strata" (a process in which managers unrelated to the original proprietors take over) about which Schumpeter wrote has hardly begun. In few companies has there been development of nonrelated management and boards of directors. In most business the family, with its myriad problems of inefficient management, still survives.

In short, the basic loyalty of the businessman is still probably to his family, only secondarily (if that) to his firm. Thus the creation of rational capitalist enterprise becomes difficult indeed when it conflicts with the noble Oriental tradition of taking care of one's family. In terms of government, the attitude in large part explains what Westerners term waste and corruption (in the shape of government payrolls padded with relatives, and so on) in many Middle Eastern countries. Those responsible see it all as the righteous way to do things. Different definitions of "venality" clearly apply.

For the past half century the mountains of Lebanon and Syria have, curiously enough, served as spawning grounds for entrepreneurship in Africa and Latin America. The phenomenon occurs as follows. The young Lebanese or Syrian male reaches the age of eighteen or twenty in his village. He wants to marry but cannot for two reasons: first, he has no job and can find none; second, the village girls his age are already spoken for by recently returned emigrants from Africa and South America, usually in the fifty-to-sixty age group. So, after two or three unsuccessful job-hunts in Beirut, Tripoli, or Damascus, he, too, emigrates to Africa or South America. While there, as a businessman, he remits money to his village. Later, having made what he considers enough to live on, he returns to the Levant, marries a young girl, converts his savings to gold rachadis or sovereigns, buries these in the ground, and lives out his life — converting the gold to local currency as necessary, but seldom investing it.[9]

The Levantines who go to the coasts of Africa customarily peddle gewgaws and rose water to native citizens and gin and bitters to Europeans. Their role is strictly commercial, but they serve, according to experts on the subject, a useful function.[10] Those who go to Mexico and Central America, however, more frequently turn to industrial pursuits, often with conspicuous success. Throughout Latin America today several hundred industrial enterprises are owned and managed by so-called "Turcos" — Lebanese and Syrians. They operate steel mills in Brazil, textile ventures in Colombia, factories making tin, matches, and explosives in Bolivia. In Africa and South America, the entrepreneurs tend toward distinctly different roles.[11]

A blending of technological and managerial skill different from that of the West distinguishes industrial management in the Middle East today. A factory is never begun from the humble workshop of a Middle Eastern version of the scientist-gadgeteer who triggered so much industrial growth in the West. The technology is almost entirely imported, via sons trained abroad or through use of foreign engineers and technicians. Factory operation is still all management and risk, no invention.[12]

There is, moreover, as yet virtually no investment by local firms in applied research of the laboratory sort. During the past half decade, United States Point Four missions and the American University of Beirut have sponsored industrial research and engineering laboratories, but these are the work of foreigners, financed from abroad, and can hardly be labeled monuments to an indigenous Baconian tradition.

Nor have factory owners proved skillful at joining together in trade associations and chambers of commerce designed to promote their collective interests through grading regulations, quality restrictions for export items, standardization of sizes, and the like. Unlike Harris Tweed weavers and Lancashire spinners, whose stamps on products have symbolized accuracy for generations, manufacturers in the Arab East and Iran have, through their lack of concern for such matters, actually lost ground since 1945 in their export trade in processed food products (such as olive oil and flour) and textiles. Systematic destruction of purchaser confidence was largely to blame.

Yet concern for scientific method does express itself in the Islamic East's version of the "improving landlord." Like their counterparts in eighteenth and nineteenth century England, urban merchants and factory owners throughout the area have begun increasingly to buy farm land — in the Syrian Jezira, the Chukorova Plain in southern Turkey, the Beka'a Valley in Lebanon. Many now invest heavily in soil improvement and modern agricultural machinery. Their operations are in striking contrast with the soil-mining techniques long associated with Middle Eastern farming.

One case is illustrative. A large Syrian textile operator has systematically transferred, since 1950, the bulk of his investments in cotton mills to farmland. His farms are "models" in the Western sense and include controlled experiments in grassland agriculture, deep well irrigation, improved conditions for peasant workers, and the rest. Moved by self-interest and the search for profit, he has probably bettered conditions for his peasants essentially to promote his own long-term survival. He also sent his two sons abroad to study. One learned agriculture in America and the other read modern history at Cambridge. Both are now back in Syria, operating the farms and helping to transplant Western ideas ranging from nitrogen fixation to the pros and cons of primogeniture into a society already changing at breakneck speed.

The family's attitudes toward Islamic inheritance practices are essentially heretical. As now planned, the family lands will be kept intact by agreements guaranteeing that one son will operate the estates as a unit. This understanding, an earlier version of which thirty years ago forced the individual in question to leave the farm to seek an urban occupation, is increasingly common in Syria, Turkey, and Iraq today. It is taking shape as the Middle East's version of the eighteenth century British practice of having one son run the estate, while the others went off to the army, the church, and to commerce.

The experience of this family, devout Moslems, also illuminates the problems facing the scholar formulating a "religion and the rise of capitalism" argument for the Middle East, based on the premise that the Moslem faith inhibits capitalistic enterprise as the Catholic Church purportedly did in medieval Europe. While interesting and provocative, the thesis is hard to illustrate and impossible to prove for the countries in question. In half-Christian, half-Moslem Lebanon, for example, most industrialists are Christians; in Syria (which is ten per cent Christian) almost all are Moslems; in Cyprus (twenty per cent Moslem) most are Christians; Moslems predominate in Turkey, Iran, Egypt, and Iraq; examples abound of highly efficient ventures owned and managed by Moslems.

Nor do divisions within Islam offer grounds for a coherent statement of a similar thesis. In the northern Persian Gulf communities, much producing (for example, small factories, boat building) and maritime enterprise is in the hands of Sunni Moslems, while the inland, pastoral Arabs are mostly Shia. Yet in Bahrein more Shiis than Sunnis are engaged in so-called "capitalist" undertakings. Turkey, considered by many a showcase for economic development in the Middle East, is mostly Sunni. Iran is a Sha nation. Ismaili Moslem communities throughout south Asia and Africa are citadels of aggressive capitalist behavior. So far, adherents of the ultra-conservative Ibhadi sect in Oman have shown little predilection for enterprise other than tweaking the tail of the British lion. Just as industrialization in Catholic Belgium and northern Italy confounds those who seek explanation for economic growth in Protestant-Catholic outlooks, the behavior of sects within Islam permits no coherent generalization.

Neither does Islamic doctrine. Indeed, the annual pilgrimage to Mecca, one of the pillars of the religion, has long served as a stimulus to capital accumulation — in the hands of those saving to make the hajj to Mecca and in the hands of the merchants, hotel owners, and transport operators who line the routes of, and milk savings from, the pilgrims. While Islam, like Christian doctrine in an earlier era, prohibits interest-taking within the Moslem community, the prohibition means as little today as it did to fourteenth century Western Christendom. To the businessman, "ribih" has come to mean profit, and interest on loans is conveniently disguised under the heading. Fatwas from the Azhar in Cairo have likewise in recent years tended to adapt the Islamic community to the requirements of an expanding capitalism. Islamic inheritance tenets — which admittedly encourage overfragmentation and hamper economic development — can be circumvented. This holds true for most of the area.

So too, strangely enough, do many of the foregoing conclusions when applied to private entrepreneurial behavior in Israel. The Western observer, conditioned to think of the ten-year-old state as being "in" the Middle East but not "of" it in terms of its institutions, intellectual infrastructure, and loyalty patterns, is amazed to note striking similarities. A team of American economic advisers to the government of Israel put the problem, two years ago, in these terms:

The lack of managerial and supervisory skill reflected the lack of experience in many fields and the difficulty and cost of acquiring such knowledge and skill through partnership, licensing and technical assistance arrangements with foreign firms, or the employment in key spots of experienced foreign personnel. In part, it may possibly have reflected a lack of appreciation of the deficiencies. High labor costs in part reflected the high degree of job security which, while socially admirable, made it difficult to reduce excessive work forces or to eliminate inefficient workers. They also reflected the absence of adequate incentive to or rewards for superior efficiency or performance. In part, high wage rates represented an effort on the part of labor to capture an amount of product which the economy simply was not producing. The absence of competition was a result in part of the virtually complete protection from foreign competition afforded by import and exchange controls and the manner in which they were administered. In part, it was the result of a widespread practice among producers and sellers operating under so-called "cartel" agreements and other similar arrangements to prevent price and other competition and to restrict production. In fact, these arrangements and the general absence of competition reflected the reluctance of the society to penalize inefficiency or to put a premium on aggressive effort.[13]

Other observers of events in Israel point to further elements of similarity in the entrepreneurship patterns of Israel and her Islamic neighbors. First there is said to be uncertainty in the minds of many industrial producers that theirs is the "good" occupation or that society really gives them credit — financially and in status — for their efforts. Next, the family firm has shown great capacity to survive, with the inevitable inefficiencies. Third, even in non-family-managed ventures, welfare state concepts often dictate that incompetent workers stay on payrolls, thus retaining the nonproductive aspects of the family firm.

Other commentators point out that fear of business failure and bankruptcy do not always work as incentives to efficient management, because chances are good that Histadrut or the central government will bail out a sinking venture. Nor, contrary to popular opinion, is the European Jew always the great entrepreneur. Israel actually inherited relatively few businessmen from western Europe. Most came from eastern and central Europe and had been conditioned by societal factors as much Eastern as Western. The really effective private enterprisers in Israel today, many claim, are Jews from South Africa.

Unfortunately the foregoing does not answer the basic question posed at the outset of the chapter. What has been said might well have applied to Naples in 1450, Cadiz in 1550, London in 1650, and possibly Boston in 1750. And it refers essentially to problems besetting those who are re-

sponsible for about twenty per cent of the annual investment in Israel, Iraq, and Iran, fifty per cent in Turkey, and
eighty per cent in Lebanon and Syria — very roughly, a
total of about $360 million out of an investment total of
just under $1 billion. Yet the same forces which shape pri-
vate entrepreneurs' decisions also affect public decision
makers, those who run governments and the development
plans. To this extent the observations may have broader
validity, but extraordinary claims should not be made.

The big unanswered question of course is still this —
what is the relation between the spirit of enterprise and the
noneconomic loyalties and actions of the enterprisers? Increasingly, industrialists are entering parliaments and are
challenging landlords and merchants as makers of public
policy. Small-scale Middle Eastern versions of Britain's corn
law controversy are very much a part of the area's politics
today. The economic facts of life presumably make the
industrialists more "public spirited" than the trader or landlord: schools and a pure water supply mean taxes, but
they also mean a healthy and more productive labor force.
(Significantly, to date the only substantial local gifts to the
ninety-two-year-old American University of Beirut, for
example, have been from "industrial" businessmen.) Will,
in short, the evolution of enterprise in the Middle East produce a counterpart for the woolsack under the lord chancel-
lors of the parliaments of Britain? Can it help narrow the
gulf between rich and poor and promote political stability?

# IV

## Cyprus

**THE "COPRA-BOAT" ECONOMY**

There's another little baby Queen Victoria has got,
Another little colony, although she's got a lot,
Another little island, very wet and very hot,
*Whatever* will we do with little Cyprus?

One idea is to make it happy with British income tax,
And another is to send a "Woolwich Infant"
With some powder and some balls,
And if they're good we'll send a minor Canon of St. Paul's
To blow the wicked up in little Cyprus.

Whatever will we do with little Cyprus. . .[1]

These lines, from an English music hall tune of the 1890's,
describe vividly the British government's frustration with
events in Cyprus from 1955 to the granting of guarantees of
independence in 1959. The mixture of Greek Cypriot demands for union with Greece, the Atlantic Alliance's strategic military involvements in the eastern Mediterranean,
the anti-Greek revival in Turkey, EOKA terrorism, com-
munal outbreaks between the island's Greek and Turkish
communities, and mounting tension between mainland
Greeks and Turks left a legacy which the republic of Cyprus will find troublesome indeed.

But disregarding the island's political contortions, Cyprus

stands today as a sobering economic artifact — far removed from the models envisioned by economists for the under-developed areas. More important, it differs greatly from the pattern sought by thoughful Westerners as fruit of an enduring East-West relationship.The structure of its econ-omy, and its recent economic history, stand as warning to nearby Middle Eastern countries, many of them equipped with similar resources, populations, and other ingredients for economic growth.

Put more concretely, Cyprus today lives from a "copra-boat" economy; like the coconut-producing islands in the Pacific, it is almost totally dependent upon outside elements for survival. Seventy-five years of rule by a Western na-tion, in this instance Britain, has not set off the self-gen-erating economic revolutions which developed Britain, America, and northern Europe. Without income from copper ore, military expenditures, tourism, and emigrant remittances, Cyprus would be economically desolate. Its economy offers an admirable capsule example of a Middle Eastern country striving to mount the launching pad of lasting economic expansion. Yet despite Western tutelage and a ten-year boom, it has so far proved incapable of the effort. The failure, while not entirely the fault of the West, is distinctly not in the West's good interests in the mid-twentieth century.[2]

Elaboration of this thesis can best be begun by recount-ing the dreary details of demography. In 1900 there were about 237,000 Cypriots on the island, today there are 544,000. Population has increased by natural means at a growing rate, beginning at about one per cent in the early years and, under stimulus of malaria control, clean water supplies, and better public-health medicine (the island's death rate is only 7 per 1000 — it was 17 per 1000 as recently as 1930), rising to just under two per cent in recent years.

As elsewhere in the Middle East, all figures in this department lead upward. By the turn of the century, if things go on like this, Cyprus will contain a million people, a fact best appreciated by those who have lived on an aircraft carrier.

There is not enough land. Despite substantial acreage improvements wrought by British Crown Colony agriculturists — land under cultivation increased forty per cent between 1930 and 1946 — the island has run out of cultivable soil, and today there are less than 1.5 acres per Cypriot. Each year the ratio worsens. Only 46,000 of the island's 940,000 cultivable acres are pump-irrigable, because of severe water shortages.

Worse yet, the land is not very good. Eroded, mined by destructive farming practices, possessed of a porous substructure which drains most of the winter rainfall into the sea, the island's wheatland yields an average of only fifteen bushels per acre. Terraced hillsides produce olives and grapes, the oil and juices of which are barely competitive with the second-grade output of Greece and Italy. Carobs and oranges alone are economically viable crops, and each year the island earns a substantial return from exporting the pods and fruit to England.

Nor is the weather on Cyprus conducive to really productive agriculture. Lying tantalizingly close (within eyeshot on clear days) to the eastern Mediterranean weather belt, where Sahara winds intersect with continental cold air masses to create 35–40 inches of rainfall yearly, most of Cyprus gets only 15 inches of moisture, all of it in midwinter, and experiences severe rainfall shortages at least once in five years. Summers are hot and dry, and from May to September dessicating winds cut soil humidity, oxidize fertilizers, erode the land, and generally impede agricultural output.

The folkways of Cypriot farmers further inhibit agricultural prosperity. By clinging tenaciously to premedieval two-field agriculture (which keeps half the island's wheatland fallow each year) and by refusing to grow cereals and animals on the same acreage, the Cypriot farmer, while increasing his numbers, has declined to embrace the simplest changes upon which soil improvement and diversified farming rest.

Cypriot farmers, the eighty per cent of them who are Greek Christians and the twenty per cent who are Turkish Moslems, have embraced Islamic inheritance practices with equally tenacious enthusiasm. The result is the standard Middle Eastern pattern of overfragmented holdings. Today the average Cypriot farm family owns 15 acres (half of which lies fallow each year), spread over an average of 12½ widely separated plots; it takes half the farmer's working day to walk between them. With each male death in rural Cyprus the situation worsens. As the island has no major cash crop such as cotton, overconcentrated holdings and sharecropping have not developed. The pattern remains one of minute subsistence holdings.

Under these circumstances, rural Cyprus has kept afloat on two liferafts. One is the move of rural Cypriots to the island's six district towns and the resultant emigration of at least 3000 yearly abroad, mostly to England. This practice had begun in earnest by 1921, at which time the island's rural population touched 250,000. Today, rural Cyprus contains about the same number, and the burgeoning district towns and overseas Cypriot communities have drained off the increase. Another is the grain subsidy, a World War II practice which has since become a permanent fixture. The Crown Colony paid Cypriot farmers (in mid-1958) $115 per ton for wheat which it could import for about $80 per ton. The total amount of the grain subsidy rose steadily after 1945. In 1957 it exceeded $2 million.

During the 1920's and 1930's, emigration to England and Commonwealth countries unquestionably was Cyprus' most effective safety valve. Like nearby eastern Mediterranean Levantines, Cypriots seemingly possess strong family and village loyalties. And their departures — for Soho and Kensington, where many became tradesmen, waiters, and restaurateurs — not only eased population pressure but established a significant flow of emigrant remittances back to the island. By 1957 capital movements to Cyprus from overseas emigrants totaled almost $10 million — $20 for every man, woman, and child on the island.

Before 1940, industry showed scant response to the increasing urban population, except in small-scale service ventures, mostly transport repair shops and the like, and in the manufacture of beverages, hard and soft. Bottling plants for flavored soda water and brandy and wines sprang up throughout the island. The two decades before 1940 served, as one observer put it, "as a warm-up period for the Cyprus beverage industry's 'finest hour,' 1957, when, in 12 months, it enveigled Cypriots to gulp down 12 cases, 144 bottles, of carbonated water per capita — plus an untold quantity of wine and cognac." Prewar expansion of other domestic-owned industry was negligible.

The one exception to the rule was copper mining. During the 1920's and 1930's the island's copper mines acquired a momentum lost in the third millennium before Christ. Working the original Mavrovouni mine of antiquity, the Mudd interests (a Los Angeles firm of mine operators and investors) developed in these years a stake originally negotiated in 1905. Faced with low copper prices before 1940, and the need to install an expensive plant on the island for reduction of cupreous and iron pyrites, the Cyprus Mines Corporation devoted most of its earnings before World War II to plant and mine development. Its payments to

shareholders and to the Crown Colony in these years were
modest, and its main effect on the island's economy was as
generator of employment for 500 to 1500 Cypriots, as a
model of safe, efficient mine operation, and as a potential
generator of large income once copper prices improved.
Like extractive industries generally in the underdeveloped
world, it was an island within an island so far as the local
economy was concerned.

World War II and its aftermath affected Cyprus much
as it did the rest of the Middle East. Allied troops with
money to spend moved in, base installations meant jobs and
higher income levels generally, shipping shortages and factory bombings in England created vast demand, much of it
pent up throughout the war. The result was an extraordinary economic expansion, particularly in manufacturing and
construction enterprise. Unemployment after 1950 dropped
to virtually nothing, investment levels soared, and the Cyprus economy registered extraordinary expansion — fed by
World War II savings, the Arab-Israeli war, the Korean
debacle, soaring world copper prices, five years of troubles
over Suez, and Cyprus' growing importance to Britain's
strategic aims in the eastern Mediterranean.

The extent of expansion in manufacturing, almost all of
it since World War II, is evident from a summary (see
Table 1) of the island's 1954–55 Industrial Census. The
figures given in Table 2 of net output per employee in industrial pursuits in 1950 and 1954 are likewise indicative
of the growth of Cyprus' economy. The island's two major
industries are mining and construction. Together they account for three quarters of the island's net output, employ
almost half its industrial labor force, yet account for only a
fifth of the number of industrial establishments. Half the
island's industrial workers are employed in establishments
of less than ten workers, and working proprietors make up

## Table 1

SUMMARY OF INDUSTRY ON CYPRUS, 1954–55

| Industry | Number of establish-ments | Number of persons employed | Gross output (£) | Net output (£) |
|---|---|---|---|---|
| All industries | 13,707 | 49,527 | 32,701,886 | 16,928,195 |
| Mining and quarrying | 355 | 6,716 | 9,681,070 | 8,465,918 |
| Manufacturing | 11,328 | 26,293 | 16,072,812 | 4,694,811 |
| Food manufacturing | 1,286 | 3,560 | 6,149,109 | 719,776 |
| Beverage industries | 258 | 1,361 | 1,993,868 | 674,400 |
| Tobacco manufacturing | 7 | 377 | 1,711,856 | 224,809 |
| Textile and clothing manufacturing | 6,694 | 11,634 | 2,498,404 | 1,076,977 |
| Wood manufacturing | 830 | 2,101 | 907,393 | 395,616 |
| Printing, publishing, and allied industries | 86 | 734 | 392,670 | 222,991 |
| Nonmetallic mineral products | 305 | 1,606 | 622,798 | 351,815 |
| Metal products | 637 | 1,657 | 570,635 | 363,035 |
| Transport equipment | 421 | 1,438 | 378,332 | 280,542 |
| Other manufactures | 804 | 1,825 | 847,747 | 384,850 |
| Construction [a] | 2,006 | 15,611 | 6,330,118 | 3,220,196 |
| Public utilities | 18 | 907 | 617,886 | 547,270 |

Source: Government of Cyprus, Census of Industry (Nicosia, 1956).
[a] The figures for construction do not include the activities of H. M. Services, either direct or through large contractors.

about a quarter of the industrial labor force. Together the statistics denote an industrial development which could hardly be termed revolutionary but which, for Cyprus, was indeed substantial.

Increased output and earnings from copper ore and cupreous and iron pyrites were the most striking elements in the island's postwar industrial expansion. By 1950 Cyprus was exporting mineral products worth more than $30 million yearly — mostly to western Europe — and the principal producer of these, the Cyprus Mines Corporation, was paying annual tax-royalties which in some years exceeded

Table 2

CYPRUS' NET ANNUAL OUTPUT PER INDUSTRIAL EMPLOYEE
(dollars)

| Industry | 1950 | 1954 |
|---|---|---|
| Mining and quarrying | 764 | 1,261 |
| Food manufacturing | 247 | 202 |
| Beverage industries | 552 | 490 |
| Tobacco manufacturing | 446 | 590 |
| Textile and clothing manufacturing | —— | 92 |
| Wood manufacturing | 98 | 188 |
| Printing and publishing | 328 | 304 |
| Nonmetallic mineral plants | 179 | 218 |
| Metal products | —— | 220 |
| Transport equipment | 168 | 196 |
| Other manufactures | —— | 210 |
| Construction | 148 | 206 |
| Public utilities | 379 | 630 |
| Average for manufacturing [a] | —— | 178 |
| Average for all industries | —— | 343 |

Source: Government of Cyprus, Census of Industry (Nicosia, 1956).
[a] Excluding mining, construction, and public utilities.

$9 million. Spurred by fifty cents a pound for copper —
an unheard-of price during the 1930's — CMC and the
island's other mining companies (some of them Greek-
owned) together gradually came to employ more than 6000
workers and to pay about a third of the Crown Colony's
operating budget.

During the decade 1946 to 1956 the Crown Colony Secretariat installed a ten-year development plan which spent
about $30 million on social overhead improvements. These
funds went for an electricity grid, improved highways and
communications facilities, better drinking water in the villages, improved public-health medicine, and a highly effec-

tive malaria eradication venture. Despite its essentially un-
coordinated nature — it was an eclectic proposition advanced by Secretariat department heads — the plan added
measurably to the island's economic infrastructure and
served as vehicle for much private enterprise activity in the
decade.

While the 1946–1956 ten year plan went ahead, United
Kingdom Treasury transfers to the island mushroomed with
the growing importance of Cyprus to the British military
establishment. Net capital transfer totals are given in Table
3. Approximately 50 per cent was spent on works projects

Table 3

NET CAPITAL TRANSFERS FROM THE UNITED KINGDOM
TREASURY TO CYPRUS

| Year | Millions of dollars | Millions of pounds |
|------|---------------------|--------------------|
| 1950 | 4.0 | 1.45 |
| 1951 | 6.6 | 2.36 |
| 1952 | 11.6 | 4.16 |
| 1953 | 12.1 | 4.33 |
| 1954 | 18.8 | 6.73 |
| 1955 | 56.2 | 20.10 |
| 1956 | 56.8 | 20.31 |
| 1957 | 58.2 | 20.80 |

Source: Government of Cyprus, Financial Secretariat.

(construction materials, labor, machinery), 15 per cent on
civilian pay (to British workers and Cypriots), 25 per cent
on soldiers' pay for spending on the island, and 10 per cent
for direct service expenditure. These funds complemented
the public outlays of the ten year plan and provided motive
force for expansion of industry and construction.

As elsewhere in the underdeveloped world, construction
showed the most rapid increase. From negligible figures

prior to World War II, building came to employ almost 20,000 men by 1958. Approximately two thirds of these were workers directly or indirectly (like a subcontractor's staff) employed on air-base or other British military projects. The remaining third worked for local contractors building civilian housing in the six district towns — most of it calculated for rental to British service families or to Cypriots with incomes expanded from association with the military establishment.

Tourism likewise grew after World War II. Blessed with a set of minor ruins covering the standard Middle Eastern time chart from Neolithic to Ottoman times, Cyprus offered a pleasant climate to the rubble-probing Englishman, philhellenes pondering which beach spawned the Goddess of Love, or the litterateur contemplating Othello's castle at Famagusta. The mountains of the Troodos range offered sanctum to honeymooning Israelis and vacationing Arabs, escaping the eastern shore summer heat in a country made cheap by British-enforced price control. By 1955, before political troubles canceled tourism entirely, travelers left almost $6 million yearly on the island.

Under the combined stimulus of a wave of capital transfers from abroad, which reached $80 million yearly by 1955 ($56 million from the United Kingdom treasury, $9 million from tax-royalty on copper sales, $9 million from emigrant remittances, $6 million from tourism), Cyprus amassed an impressive set of statistics of economic growth. These figures, partially derivative from the $150 per Cypriot pumped into the economy each year from outside and partially attributable to the island's capitalist inclinations, afford a distinctly cheery appearance.

Cyprus' national income grew, between 1950 and 1957, from about $98 million to more than $212 million. In current prices this meant more than a doubling of the per capita

income — from about $175 in the former year to almost
$380 in the latter. During the interval, however, prices rose
54 per cent and population increased at an average rate of
1 ¾ per cent yearly. The island's net advance in national
income, expressed in per capita terms, averaged out, therefore, to about 5 per cent yearly after 1950. By any standards, American, European, or Asian, the rate of increase has
been impressive.

So, too, are figures related to savings and investment.
Gross investment in 1950, for example, totaled almost $15
million, 17 per cent of national income. By 1957 the figure
reached $55 million, about 25 per cent of national income.
These rates, high by any standards, exceed even those of
most Western nations. On the basis of crude capital-output
ratio measurements, investment levels have been adequate
to advance per capita incomes at extraordinary rates.

Cyprus has in recent years run a substantial deficit in its
international trade balance. This totals $40 million to $60
million yearly — a figure which each year is redressed by
the United Kingdom treasury transfers discussed above.
Economists pay little attention to the figures. First of all,
the deficit is essentially a record of the cost of maintaining
the British military force on the island and does not represent an actual difference between what Cypriots buy and
sell abroad. And second, because of sterling area controls,
the unfavorable exchange ratios besetting countries with
chronic balance of payments difficulties (like Turkey and
Israel) have not come to Cyprus. Even the political disturb-
ances have been insufficient to upset the Cyprus pound in
Zurich, Beirut, and Tangier. The island's balance of payments for 1956 and 1957 is contained in Table 4.

The Cyprus pound indeed has remained stable throughout the past decade and has fluctuated in world markets only
to the extent of shifts in the value of the sterling pound.

Table 4

Cyprus' Balance of Payments, 1956 and 1957
(millions of pounds)

| Item | 1956 | | 1957 [a] | |
|---|---|---|---|---|
| | *Receipts* | *Payments* | *Receipts* | *Payments* |
| Goods and services: | | | | |
| Merchandise (adjusted) [b] | 22.21 | 34.22 | 18.97 | 39.46 |
| Nonmonetary gold | c | c | c | c |
| Foreign travel | 1.23 | 1.08 | 1.10 | 1.50 |
| Transport and insurance | 1.32 | 5.61 | 1.35 | 6.45 |
| Investment income | 0.96 | 9.41 | 0.95 | 7.39 |
| Government transactions | 20.31 | 0.04 | 16.00 | 0.04 |
| Miscellaneous | 0.76 | 1.00 | 0.96 | 1.00 |
| Total | 46.79 | 51.36 | 39.33 | 55.84 |
| Donations: | | | | |
| Private | 3.10 | 0.45 | 3.10 | 0.45 |
| Official | 0.75 | c | 4.80 | c |
| Total | 3.85 | 0.45 | 7.90 | 0.45 |
| Capital: | | | | |
| Private | 1.85 | 1.99 | 1.37 | 0.51 |
| Official and banking | 4.23 | 5.67 | 4.79 | 0.30 |
| Total | 6.08 | 7.66 | 6.16 | 0.81 |
| Errors and omissions | 2.75 | 0.00 | 3.71 | 0.00 |
| Grand total | 59.47 | 59.47 | 57.10 | 57.10 |

Source: *Cyprus Economic Review, 1957* (Nicosia, 1958).
[a] Provisional.
[b] "Merchandise (adjusted)" differs from trade account figures because imports are adjusted by deducting freight and insurance charges and exports by deducting ships' stores. These items are included in "Transport and insurance."
[c] Negligible amount.

Unlike other sterling area members, some of whom have carried out devaluation since 1949, the sterling backing of the Cyprus pound has been added to consistently for ten years. In mid-1958 the Cyprus currency issue was backed by 104 per cent sterling, and it has withstood apparent balance of payments deficits and political troubles most adequately.

The foregoing paragraphs would seem to contradict the

gloomy prophecy contained at the outset of this essay. They
bear out the theme of unqualified optimism accompanying
most statements on the island's economy.[3] What, then, is
the basis for pessimism regarding Cyprus' future? Reasons
follow:

First, despite ten years of expansion, the island's national
income still shows the customary lopsided distribution common to underdeveloped areas. Per capita incomes earned
from farming in Cyprus still average about $150 — less than
half the annual incomes produced in mining, industry, and
the distributive trades. Yet half the island's populace is rural
and essentially dependent on agriculture for a living. Increases, moreover, in rural income have lagged far behind
those in urban occupations. The Cypriot farmer is simply
not a candidate to buy increased output from industrial
plants.

Nor can the Cypriot farmer squeeze enough from his
meager output to invest in soil improvement or the other
avenues to really increased production. His main investment, to date, has been to let half his land lie fallow each
year. (Conservationists estimate that nature requires roughly
two hundred years to replace an inch of topsoil under this
system.) He cannot, for many reasons, make the transition
into heavier investment and more diversified agriculture.

Breakdown of the island's figures of investment is illustrative. In 1957 (a typical year), only 13 per cent of investment funds flowed into agriculture and mining. The re-
mainder was divided almost equally between machinery
purchased abroad (much of which was transport machinery) and investment in housing and buildings. While Cyprus invests therefore at an extraordinarily high percentage
of national income (20–25 per cent), a fact to delight those
who play with capital-output ratios, probably too much
goes into housing and trucks and spare parts and factory

machinery bought abroad. And too little goes into mining and agriculture — the backbone of the island's economy.

Investment in housing is confined, moreover, almost exclusively to luxury flats and apartments in the six district towns. No funds flow into improving rural homes, and the urban housing is designed essentially for occupancy by foreigners or by upper-income Cypriots.

Even worse, the island's copper is running out. At present rates of extraction (almost a million tons of five per cent ore are currently being processed annually) Cyprus copper producers will be forced to work low-grade ore within five years. Proved reserves do not point to further seams remotely comparable to the Mavrovouni mine. While forecasts of tax-royalty income from copper exports are approximations at best, it is not unreasonable to expect these incomes to halve (particularly in view of dropping world copper prices), from $9 million to less than $5 million in a few years.

Fourth, the British Government announced (prior to the Middle East troubles in the summer of 1958) its intention of cutting back its military expenditures on the island from an estimated $56 million in 1957 to about $45 million in 1958, with further reductions scheduled for future years. An inevitable accompaniment to this would be decreased investment in housing, rising unemployment as some of the 8,000–12,000 base workers became redundant, and lower incomes to service industries (automobile rental, beverage manufacture, entertainment) dependent on troops for sustenance. Unemployment reached 9,500 by mid-1959.

Next, no way has yet been found for Cypriot merchants to enter the East-West entrepôt trade. Skill at this has long kept nearby Lebanon solvent despite its meager resources, lack of industry, and overpopulation. Yet the ships sail by Cyprus, many within eyeshot, and Cypriots gain negligible income from the cargoes. For their plight in this respect (as in most others) Cypriots blame Britain — for failing to build a really good deep-water port and free zone on the island and for enforcing sterling area exchange controls, which prevent the fast and elaborate transactions associated with East-West trade and its finance.

Colonial administrators on the other hand labeled the Cypriots' ineptness as entrepreneurs one reason for the island's exclusion from entrepôt trade. They pointed to the paucity of really well run enterprises, primitive bookkeeping techniques, payrolls packed with relatives, and the other elements of business in a preindustrial society as basic reasons for Cyprus' commercial isolation. The fact is, the Cypriot entrepreneur has probably gone about as far as he can, given the raw material costs and purchasing power available to him.

Sixth, seventy-five years of rule by a Western nation failed to launch Cyprus into an interlocking agricultural and industrial revolution. Poor soil, overfragmentation, lack of investment, and Cypriot farmers' folkways join to make rural Cyprus incapable today of producing raw materials for urban industry or of buying factory goods. The island's industry lives essentially from selling to British forces or to Cypriots deriving income from HMG's base expenditures. Rural Cyprus lives from the grain subsidy and by exporting Cypriots.

The Colonial Office ten year plan, in many ways an admirable effort, set out only to improve the island's power sources, communications, cooperatives, transport, and public health. These public investments, complemented by a monetary policy linking the Cyprus pound to sterling, undeniably made a vehicle for much of the decade's economic growth. But the plan did not succeed in altering investment directions from housing and transport machinery into agri-

culture and mining. Nor did it really attack problems resulting from overfragmentation of land. Neither did it result in
a useful deep-water port — troop movements for the Suez
landings, for example, were largely mounted from Malta.
Finally, the plan did not enunciate a mining lease policy
designed to encourage search for new ore bodies on the
island. Exploration by copper concerns has, in view of the
Secretariat's vagueness on future lease policy, been desul-
tory for an entire decade.

Yet failure of the ten year plan to flood Cyprus with
enduring prosperity cannot be laid solely at the feet of the
British Colonial Office. Coordinated economic planning,
still admittedly in its infant stages and as yet essentially unproved, began in capitalist countries only after World War
II. Cyprus first needed an adequate set of public utilities,
and installation of these occupied the island's administrators
and took most of its excess revenues from 1946 to 1956.
Postwar Britain was financially incapable, had it wanted to,
of launching an American-type aid program (as in Puerto
Rico) for Cyprus. Following Commonwealth policy, each
unit in the empire was expected to "pay its own way." Cyprus did this, and its copper revenues were spent on the
island with a minimum of what, on Middle Eastern standards, would pass for "corruption."

The economy of Cyprus takes shape, therefore, as one
pulled to unnaturally high levels by international disaster,
yet increasingly dependent upon copper exports, military
bases, emigrant remittances, and tourism — all essentially
external in nature — for sustenance. From its pre-World
War II status as "Cinderella of the British Empire," Cyprus
has come to practice a form of inverse imperialism in which
it exacts a high price indeed, from the West, for its geographic position, minerals, and family loyalties. Population
pressure has long since overstrained the island's resources,

and Cypriots' living standards undeniably have reached unnaturally high levels under stimulus of its peculiar role in the world. Meanwhile, the specter of dropping income from copper sales and military base outlays is a constant threat.

What should be done? Put in general terms, the answer seems disarmingly simple. First, ways must be found for Cyprus to continue to sell itself as home for Western military establishments, for the highest price possible. As a paratroop police station for troubles elsewhere in the Middle East, Cyprus is still distinctly useful to the Atlantic Alliance. Next, the island's government should enunciate a mining lease policy so attractive that widespread exploration would commence and continue. Third, construction of a deepwater port and a program to urge Cypriot merchants into the East-West trade should be tried as companion programs. Fourth, the emigration of Cypriots should be encouraged, and those who go should receive all stimulus to return often, to keep family ties active and the flow of remittances high. Finally, tourism should be developed and expanded.

Implementation of the above measures probably can come only from a coordinated economic development plan, like Puerto Rico's, designed to help change the island's historic investment directions and ultimately the basic structure of its economy. Unless more funds go into Cyprus' main pillars of sustenance — agriculture, mining, tourism, nonconstruction industry — the island cannot hope to check the vicious circle of low purchasing power inhibiting increased output which afflicts it and most of the underdeveloped world today.

To achieve dramatic results, such a plan would doubtless require far greater resources, natural, human, and financial, than are currently available. Cypriots' mental attitudes would need to change radically — views toward agricul-

tural production, business management, savings and investment, and the like. More land under irrigation and increased
output from *all* land are essential. More funds for investment than those currently available — from private savings,
taxes, and investment — must be found, probably through
foreign aid.

Yet the best plan for Cyprus, with adequate funds, would
still depend for lasting success on yet unknown breakthroughs in technology. When experiments in arid-zone
agriculture produce really effective low-rainfall grasses, the
island can try mixed farming on a major scale. With cheap
power from the sun, heavy water, or whatever makes sea-
water distillation economically practicable, Cyprus can increase its irrigated acreage and farm production immensely.
But until discoveries such as these occur, there must be well
defined limits on the island's potential for economic growth,
and a plan would be a distinctly long-risk proposition.

Meanwhile the boom of the past decade is definitely running down. Since mid-1958, unemployment figures have
risen, investment in really productive enterprise is microscopic, copper prices are down, British military expenditures have begun to slacken. Despite tutelage by a Western
nation, substantial foreign exchange from copper exports,
minimal "corruption" in the expenditure of public funds,
and huge outlays by the British military establishment, Cyprus is still economically unviable and a ward of the West
for its food and clothing. This result of seventy-five years'
mixing of Western rule with Middle Eastern resources —
natural and human — is distinctly sobering and, one hopes,
*not* symptomatic of inevitable developments elsewhere in
the Middle East.

# V

## Turkish Land Reform

### AN EXPERIMENT IN MODERATION

The only defensible generalization about Middle Eastern farmland today is that it is owned and worked in parcels too large or too small to benefit most of the area's citizens. So far nothing resembling the patterns of northern Europe and North America — which, while varying widely, have achieved high levels of output per acre of land *and* per worker — has evolved. Most students of the subject place land use today near the top of the list of obstacles to economic development in the Middle East.[1]

Abundant statistical evidence supports the view. In pre-revolution Egypt less than twelve thousand families owned more than a third of the country's six million cultivable acres, while almost fifteen million Egyptians lived from sharecropping or freehold farming on plots too small to be economically viable. About the same percentages apply to Pakistan, Iran and Iraq, Syria and Lebanon. Turkey at the end of World War II considered that half its 2.5 million farm families owned either no land or parcels too small for livelihood, while several hundred establishments used share-cropping methods for land in excess of 1,000 acres.[2] Under these circumstances, "citizenship of the soil," effective demand from farm families, and the other ingredients of lasting economic growth simply are not there.

Those parts of the Islamic Middle East practicing settled agriculture — Turkey, Egypt, Iran, the northern Arab countries — reveal pretty much the broad historical pattern of the evolution of land problems. Briefly put, this consists of the superimposition of the modern nation state on the chaotic foundations built by nineteenth century Ottoman land policy. Twentieth century nationhood congealed, by affording it legal title, a set of untenable arrangements derived from the Sipahilik system, from Ottoman land laws of 1858 and after, and from an emergent "feudalism" with few of the redeeming virtues of its European namesake. Control of land passed in the process to large landlords (former Ottoman functionaries and in some instances shaikhs who took personal title to tribal dirahs), to Islamic wakfs, and to the state. Peasant rights varied widely, but sharecropping was the customary mode of production. Where peasants did acquire firm title, plots were customarily tiny.[3]

Twentieth century nationhood brought with it, and was in some cases preceded by, cotton production. In Egypt, for example, cotton growing served to introduce one more oppressor to the Middle Eastern peasant — the uncertainties of the world fiber and textile market. Cotton growing undeniably furthered expansion of overconcentrated holdings. So too did the post-1900 population explosion. Elsewhere, the decline of the Persian rug industry after World War I, the area's steadily worsening demographic position, establishment by the British raj of "Jagir" estates in the Punjab, all furthered the same process. In many cases urban merchants joined traditional landowners as holders of soil, villages, and, for practical purposes, the humans in them.

The area's religions probably promoted the process. Islamic theology, through its hold on poorer, inevitably worse educated farmers, encouraged division of holdings at death among wives and surviving male heirs. Eastern orthodox

Christianity, the area's second rural religion, offered no alternative to Islamic inheritance practices. Moslem-like overfragmentation has broken up the holdings of its adherents in Cyprus and the mountains of Lebanon. Larger owners, Moslem and Christian, have avoided this by primogeniture-like arrangements which retained holdings in economically feasible units. But the vast majority of Middle Eastern farmers for generations engaged in overfragmentation.

Low output per worker, coupled with lack of incentive all around, customarily accompanies both extremes of Middle East land tenure. The sharecropping peasant who produces more wheat, rice, or cotton knows that the larger share will inevitably go to the landowner or moneylender. The small freeholder, saddled with debt already, knows that the price of cash advances will adjust with alacrity to his added affluence — as seemingly do crop failure, insect invasions, and the other natural regulators of life in the rural Middle East. Landlords, after achieving a certain scale (which varies widely throughout the area, from fifty acres in the Nile delta to fifty villages in dry-farming Iran), do well from low output of large areas of land and many peasants.

Few other area-wide generalizations about Middle East land tenure are permissible. The systems have, for example, led to widely variant land productivity. Egypt produces more cotton per acre than any land in the world — except, perhaps, the Imperial Valley in California; yet the rest of the Islamic Middle East averages seven to ten bushels of wheat per acre plus correspondingly low figures for cotton and other cash crops.

Investment in land, both in its purchase and its improvement, likewise varies widely. For almost a century Egypt has invested its surpluses almost solely in land and, to a lesser extent, in land improvement — irrigation, drainage, fertilizers. The Pashas, while doing little else to recommend themselves, did maintain the deep alluvial topsoil of the Nile Valley surprisingly well. The rest of the Islamic Middle East has mined the soil systematically. In Cyprus and Anatolia and from the eastern Mediterranean to the Punjab a major economic problem has been the lack of private funds flowing into soil improvement. Public soil improvement projects, like those in Iraq and Turkey, are now beginning. But the fact remains that the largest investment put into most Middle East farmland today is still two-field rotation which permits half the land to lie fallow each year. A few improving landlords, conceivably the future "Turnip Townshends" of the Middle East, now operate farms in Lebanon, Syria, and Iraq, but their impact is still inconsequential.

A broader impact is being made by the multitude of programs in land reform begun since World War II by almost every Middle Eastern government. Most are drastic, and follow the lead of Egypt. Egypt's republican government in 1952 decreed a top limit of about 200 acres per owner, while simultaneously enunciating bond schemes for compensation, resettlement of landless peasants, and consolidation of fragmented plots and cooperatives to cement the undertaking. On 27 September 1958 Syria passed a similar reform law, calling for top limits of 200 acres for irrigated land and 750 acres for rainfall-watered areas, with compensation payable over forty years through $1\frac{1}{2}$ per cent interest bonds. Four days later, on 1 October 1958, Iraq's revolutionary government issued a law confiscating — with compensation over twenty years at 3 per cent — all holdings over 250 acres (1000 dunams) if irrigated, and 500 acres (2000 dunams) if rainfall-watered.[4] The military government in Pakistan issued similar decrees a few weeks later. All are now undergoing implementation with varying degrees of severity.

Accurate evaluation of the drastic schemes for land reform is still, at this early date, a hopeless task. Intriguing conjecture goes on, but nobody has yet presented really definitive evidence of the program's effects on income, incentives, production, investment, wealth, and industrial growth.[5] Against this backdrop, therefore, land reform as tried in Turkey since 1945 becomes increasingly relevant. Turkey's program has been a moderate one and its accomplishments and failures are now visible.[6]

When the Grand National Assembly passed the first land distribution law on 11 June 1945, Turkey knew little about its land ownership, productivity, or rural conditions generally.[7] It was evident that these needed improving. For despite a usable land area of more than 145 million acres and a post-World War II population of just under 19 million — 7 acres per citizen — Turkey in 1945 still imported grain and dairy products to feed her cities.[8] Rural Turkey, moreover, suffered from a wretched road system, few farmers could market their crops, and the purchasing power of Anatolian and Thracian peasants was indescribably low. Ataturk's reforms of the between-wars decades had, except for occasional teachers and village school houses, by-passed rural Turkey.

Turkey's land law was designed to be partially corrective, partially preventive. The country needed more farm products — food and industrial raw materials. Obviously more land had to be farmed. In some areas concentrated ownership and sharecropping were problems, yet most farmers seemingly owned their own land. The law's initial intent was to eliminate the large estates and sharecropping while increasing the small farmers' holdings and cementing their position in the face of the nation's planned spurts of economic growth. The yeoman farmer was part of postwar Turkey's dream.

Yet, by Oriental standards, Turkish yeoman farmers had

long done well. With few exceptions, there was enough land to supply flour grain and vegetables for rural families; indeed, in good crop years an embarrassing surplus frequently rotted in the fields. For the Turkish farmer, to work longer and produce more was foolish: transport and marketing facilities were too primitive for disposal of surpluses. As a result, while peasants sat in the coffee houses, Turkey accumulated by 1945 an estimated ten million acres of unused, cultivable soil. Some was owned by the state, some by religious foundations and provincial administrations, some by nobody.

Land commissions created by the 1945 law set out to distribute these ten million acres and to confiscate and redistribute privately owned land — that in excess of 1250 acres if worked by the owner, 500 acres if sharecropped or rented. By now a common sight in Turkish villages, more than a hundred of the land commissions still operate.

Upon entering a village, the land commissions first undertake a comprehensive survey of land use and ownership, assess the condition of lands farmed by villagers, and try to establish exact title. Next, the commissions solicit applications from needy farmers, meanwhile drawing on the advice of village councils — members of which are first administered an elaborate oath to tell the truth — as to the relative affluence of villagers. Next follow public meetings, with the entire village present. This serves as a cross-check on dishonesty by applicants or village councilors. Eventually, the commissions grant title to needy villagers, frequently by drawing lots if there are disputes over particular plots.

To determine need, the land commissions employ an ingenious yardstick permitting measurement under Turkey's widely variant soil and water conditions. They have ruled that a five-person farm family needs sufficient land to produce a minimum income equivalent to the value of ten metric tons of wheat — at current world wheat prices a per capita income between $200 and $300. The commissions' estimates of annual family requirements are broken down in Table 5. Where possible, the commissions exceed mini-

Table 5

COST, IN TERMS OF KILOGRAMS OF WHEAT, OF THE ANNUAL REQUIREMENTS OF A TURKISH FAMILY OF FIVE

| Requirement | Kg of wheat |
|---|---|
| Food (300 kg per person) | 1500 |
| Seed (15 kg per decare for 200 decares) | 3000 |
| Clothing | 1400 |
| Fees (in connection with the crop) | 1000 |
| Tools and machines (maintenance and amortization) | 800 |
| Animal fodder (6 months; 3 kg of oats per day per animal) | 1080 |
| Taxes and village assessment | 1000 |
| Total [a] | 9780 |

Source: R. D. Robinson, unpublished report to the Institute of Current World Affairs, 1952.
[a] The addition of a 10% provision for drought and famine brings the total to well over ten metric tons.

mum allotments and also adjust land grants to comply with peasants' needs with different soils and rainfall. Irrigated land, for example, is assumed to produce at least four times the yield from dry farming. As shown in Table 6, allowances are also made for types of land permitting animal crop agriculture and mixed farming.

To receive land, a peasant must prove that he owns too little land or none at all, that he has studied agriculture or veterinary science, that the Ministry of Agriculture has encouraged him to become a farmer, or that he is a nomad or

Table 6

AMOUNT OF LAND REQUIRED ON A TURKISH FARM TO
PRODUCE TEN METRIC TONS OF WHEAT [a]

(decares)

| Quality of field | Dry farming | Bottom land | Irrigation possible |
|---|---|---|---|
| ARID REGION | | | |
| Poor | 400[b] | 200 | 50 |
| Average | 275 | 150 | 35 |
| Good | 150 | 100 | 20 |
| RAINY REGION | | | |
| Poor | 160 | 80 | 40 |
| Average | 110 | 60 | 30 |
| Good | 60 | 40 | 20 |

Source: R. D. Robinson, unpublished report to the Institute of Current
World Affairs, 1952.

[a] Allowing for half the land to be left fallow every year.

[b] Under these conditions average production is 50 kg per decare (about
6 bushels per acre); hence it takes 200 decares (roughly 50 acres) to
produce 10 tons of wheat, another 200 being fallowed.

migrant anxious to practice settled agriculture. He must
further agree that he or his family will work the land for
25 years, during which time he cannot sell or sharecrop it.

At present rates of distribution, Turkey's land reform
program is nearly half complete. About half of the originally earmarked 10 million acres have been distributed to
more than 250,000 families, out of an estimated recipient
list of 870,000. Figures for 1947–1955 are given in Table 7.

With Turkish land reform in mid-stream, some generalizations about it, and its relevance to other parts of the
Islamic, wheat-eating, village-living Middle East, become
practicable.

First, the Turkish government admittedly attacked its
land tenure problem in 1945 with energy and astuteness.

## Table 7

LAND DISTRIBUTED BY THE TURKISH GOVERNMENT, 1947–1955

| Year | Land distributed (decares) | Number of recipient families | Number of villages [a] | Pastureland assigned (decares) [b] |
|---|---|---|---|---|
| 1947 | 49,086 | 1,427 | 29 | 0 |
| 1948 | 238,656 | 4,313 | 110 | 0 |
| 1949 | 389,212 | 8,359 | 148 | 0 |
| 1950 | 745,671 | 18,589 | 333 | 442,196 |
| 1951 | 1,231,823 | 22,697 | 333 | 1,674,311 |
| 1952 | 1,773,552 | 41,519 | 487 | 1,265,491 |
| 1953 | 2,241,355 | 41,528 | 508 | 1,158,468 |
| 1954 | 2,539,820 | 44,850 | 475 | 1,089,479 |
| 1955 [c] | 2,043,850 | 45,301 | — | 834,591 |
| Total | 11,253,025 | 228,583 | 2,423 | 6,445,536 |

Source: R. D. Robinson, *Developments Respecting Turkey, 1955–56* (New York, 1956).

[a] Number of villages in which recipients were located.

[b] Pastureland, previously held in the name of the village, distributed to individual families.

[c] May include some 1956 distribution.

Without soliciting lengthy reports from foreign experts, the Turks passed a law that could be implemented without upsetting the nation's post-World War II political balance. Where the law was weak, it reflected the sentiment of the businessmen, professional people, and landlords who comprise its Grand National Assembly. Unlike interwar Turkey, the country is not ruled by its army. Decisive and immediate land reform by fiat simply was, and is, impossible. Ataturk's revolution probably served as a prelude to land reform in Turkey, but even the strong government of Mustapha Kemal feared to try the measures practicable in republican (but army-controlled) Egypt, Iraq, Syria, and Pakistan.

It is doubtful indeed if Turkey's land reform has played a significant role in increasing the nation's grain production.

Astounding increases have occurred during good crop years. From 1946 to 1953, for example, Turkey shifted its position from that of a wheat importer to that of the world's fourth largest exporter. Increases came mainly from additional land under cultivation, only secondarily from yield improvements. Yet these new lands would most certainly have been put to the plough regardless of ownership — under stimulus of Turkey's postwar improvements in transport and marketing, the grain subsidy, and the wildfire spread of ECA tractors. Mechanization and other factors have obscured, in short, the role of land reform in overall production.

In the matter of acres owned, Turkey's small farmers and landless peasants undeniably have benefited from the reform program. The land commissions have distributed an average of 11.5 acres per family processed. Adding this to earlier holdings, the average rural family in Turkey by 1952 was farming just under 20 acres; 93 per cent owned their own land, and less than 3 per cent of the families were sharecroppers. Seventy-five per cent of Turkey's farmers have entered, since 1952, the 20-acre group.[9] By Middle Eastern standards, this phase of the land program is remarkable.

Yet Turkey's 20-acre farmers are still a far cry from the yeomanry envisioned by postwar republican governments. Although the farmer now has security of tenure, he owns a quantity of land which under optimum dry farming conditions can still barely produce the ten tons of wheat, with its resultant per capita income of $200–$300 yearly, which Turkey employs as a norm for rural improvement. The farmer is still subject to monotonously regular crop failure. He has barely begun to rotate grasses with cereals. His animal crop agriculture is rudimentary at best, and his 20-acre parcel is still inadequate.

Indeed, Turkey's central rural problem still lies in her small farms. Surpluses for investment on the land and increased family purchasing power cannot flow automatically from 20-acre holdings. Further fragmentation, too, is a constant hazard as many illiterate marginal farmers cling to the only security they know and divide holdings — in fact if not in the registry office — among several surviving heirs.

Yet land reform has not broken up the large farms of Turkey. Although the commissions are empowered to confiscate and redistribute private holdings over 1250 acres, examples where this has occurred are rare.[10] By transferring title to sons and relatives, capitalizing on confusion over ownership inherent in Turkey since 1858, and other subterfuge, landlords have with few exceptions retained management of, if not title to, their holdings. Since 1952, almost 25 per cent of Turkey's farmers have been in the over-20-acre owner group, and less than 1 per cent of rural families still operate 20 per cent of the nation's farmland.[11]

Survival of the larger units has, like the 20-acre farm, had ambiguous effect. The 20-acre wheat farm being obviously too small to support tractors and other mechanization, most machinery has gone onto larger holdings. While absorbing the country's 40,000 tractors and keeping investment channels open for 20 per cent of the nation's farmland, Turkey's large farms have also accounted for most increases in yield per acre. From the viewpoint of production and productivity, survival of the larger units has been beneficial.

Increased yields from larger acreages, particularly in the Chukorova plain in south Turkey, have also virtually destroyed sharecropping as customarily practiced. Tractors, fertilizers, and better techniques have multiplied output. Landlords therefore have displaced former sharecroppers. Some former croppers have returned, meanwhile, as daily paid workers. Those lucky peasants who become tractor

drivers or irrigation workers do well. The displacees, however, are pathetic indeed, and the city of Adana impresses
the visitor as a symbol of both hope and tragedy.[12]

The Chukorova plain experience, in a slightly less ag-
gravated fashion, has been typical of Turkish agriculture.
Across the nation, land reform and mechanization together
have led to less sharecropping, more renting, more daily
paid farm labor, and as yet little discernible change in the
ratios of land farmed by large and small holders. Since 1952
only 4 per cent of Turkey's farmers rate as sharecroppers,
and there has been a steady rise in tenancy, custom ploughing by tractor operators, and the growth of "factories in the
fields" — all symbols, by Middle Eastern standards, of a
prospectively dynamic agriculture. Countrywide expansion
of sharecropping has clearly been checked.

The Turks undeniably have, moreover, tackled the central problem facing land reformers in underdeveloped countries — the matter of who actually owns the land. While in-
stalling the usual crop subsidies, easy credit, and other elements which elsewhere pass for rural reform, they have not
let these obscure the basic issue. Their program has fixed
legal title, distributed government and wakf-owned land,
and expanded the property base of the nation's small farmers. Where large owners have added to the acreage they
farm, it has been mostly by renting. The hold of the yeoman farmer definitely has been strengthened, and the nation's equity base broadened.

Turkish land reform has not, however, led to appreciable
redistribution of income. As mentioned earlier, confiscation
has been rare, and such redistribution as has gone on has
been within the confines of the landlord families. Yet peasant proprietors have been afforded a chance, partially by
the land laws and partially by other rural improvements,
to hitch onto Turkey's expanding economy and profit from

its growth. Landlords and peasants alike are undeniably better off today than they were a decade ago.

To date peasant affluence has not led to appreciable cash investment, by small proprietors, in Turkey's farmland. Most authorities conclude that Anatolian farmers have invested more time — hours previously spent in the village coffee house — in working their lands, some newly acquired. They have also adopted better techniques urged upon them by extension workers, and in some instances have expended part of their surplus earnings on better seeds or simple tools. But the bulk of their surplus has gone into consumption, everything from more cigarettes and sugar to better clothing, and into the traditional peasant insurance — gold rachadis for the inevitable rainy day. Cash investment in small farms has been largely at the hands of the Turkish government, through credit, machinery grants, and the rest.

Turkish land reform has proved also, along with the other heroic measures tried since 1945, to be a woefully temporary stopgap against the growing force of pressure on the land from population growth. By increasing at 3 per cent per year, Turks have cut their overall man-land ratio from seven acres per citizen to six acres in the brief span since 1950. This 17 per cent drop has by no means been offset by a corresponding increase in productivity. Improved public-health medicine and better food and clothing have heightened the nation's population pressure. Relief has come through growing migration to the cities. From 1950 to 1955 alone, Turkey's urban percentage rose 3.3 per cent — including a movement of about 800,000 people off the land. Life in the growing slums of Ankara and Istanbul seemingly offers increasing appeal to Turkey's peasants.[13] Against this tide, land reform has been a sheet anchor, not a sail.

Nor has its moderate land reform led Turkey remotely near to the rural patterns drafted by chance, the Department of Agriculture, and the New Deal in America and long before by the enclosure movement in Britain. While differing widely, these created the 160-acre farm in the midwestern United States, large estates coupled with renting farmers and daily paid workers in England — systems promoting high productivity per unit of land and labor on both sides of the Atlantic. Except for its attack on the institution of sharecropping, and definite improvement in the lot of the small farmer, common also to the American and British experience, Turkish land reform has as yet little relevance to these movements. Obviously no Turkish counterpart of Western land ownership and tenancy is yet visible. Nor will it probably appear.

Turkish land reform has undeniably accented the need for some kind of "balance" between investments in rural improvement, public-health medicine, and urban development (including industrialization) in a changing Middle East. For example, tractors alone have involved a ten-year investment of $200 million, paid for by Turkey and the United States. Despite land reform, each of the 40,000 tractors has displaced an estimated eight peasants. To reinsert these men as workers elsewhere in the economy costs from $5,000 to $10,000 per family — a total investment bill of over $2 billion, $200 million yearly. Over the last decade, Turkey has come nowhere near the latter figure. As shock-absorber for such imbalance, land reform has been a thin cushion indeed.[14]

Turkey's experience in land reform has also made clearer the relation of this measure of economic development with the other threads in the fabric. Land reform cannot create a stable yeomanry in Turkey unless there is a dramatic change in the patterns of values, levels of education, competence in technology, and other requisites of harmonious social and economic change. The Turk who burns his animal dung for fuel rather than putting it on his soil, grows no grasses on his nitrogen-hungry topsoil, lubricates his tractor improperly if at all, discourages his sons from becoming tradesmen and entrepreneurs because such occupations traditionally fell to the Christian foreigners, and divides his land at death by Islamic rather than Turkish law could only by greatest accident establish a durable productive unit for the country's rural economy.

Shifts in mental outlook and more balanced investment clearly are the keys to sustained economic advance in Turkey. With these, the country's land reform law could sustain redrafting and might, in unison with other improvements, help avert some of the suffering and turmoil associated with rural and urban growth and population shifts in the West. As he demonstrated with terrifying thoroughness in the Istanbul riots in September 1955, the displaced Turkish peasant in the mid-twentieth century will not die peacefully by the roadside as did his counterpart in seventeenth century England. His energies need constructive harnessing. Turkish land reform has helped promote the process, but incredibly much remains to be done.

# VI

## The New Capitalism

### OIL COMPANIES AS INNOVATORS

The press in England and America and reports by unin-
formed travelers have joined to implant in the Western
mind an impression best described as the "Cadillac interpretation of events in the Middle East." Western oil companies'
operations in the Middle East are pictured as transplants of
Texas and Nottinghamshire for the foreign workers, air-
conditioned company towns for local employees, fabulous
company profits and tax-royalty payments to local governments, and negligible economic growth of a "healthly" nature. Tax-royalties go, according to the argument, to governments practicing various brands of Oriental despotism,
little of the money rubs off on the mass of citizens, and,
oil company window-dressing aside, the net result of this
form of East-West cooperation is a vast phalanx of tail-
finned Cadillacs hurtling across deserts, while picturesque
shaikhs inside them fire shotguns from the windows at
gazelles.

Despite obvious distortions, frequently intentional, the
argument contains elements of truth. Until very recently,
neither oil company tax-royalty payments nor employee
wage bills and local purchasing have had much effect on
economic development. The government and shaikhs of
Saudi Arabia have, since 1946, exhibited consummate skill

at converting oil earnings into a Himalayan pile of Western-made consumers' goods, symbolized in fact and legend by the Cadillac. Iran before 1950 did much the same, albeit more discreetly — the Iranian ruling class put its money into villas in Cannes and not solely into conspicuous consumption at home. So, before the Development Board took charge of oil earnings in 1952, did Iraq. In each case the traditionalism of society joined with ineffective public administration and technically complex oil operations to prevent oil earnings from promoting broad economic development.

Before World War II oil companies themselves were little concerned with the problem. Anxious to avoid "imperialist" behavior, long anathema to Middle Easterners, company executives studiously refrained from efforts to check the flow of tax-royalties into the area's bottomless pit. Nor, needless to say, did they try to reconstruct the pit itself. The occasional purchasing officer who tried local buying of automobile spare parts, textiles, shoes, or other company needs invariably encountered — in Abadan or Baghdad — unreliable inventories, mercurial price changes, or inadequate supplies. After one or two chastening experiences, he invariably turned back to ordering supplies from the usual sources in western Europe, the United Kingdom, and America. "External economies" servicing the oil camps simply did not develop.

One example, drawn from northern Iraq, is illustrative. Oil operations have gone on near Kirkuk since the 1920's. The installations there now employ several thousand workers, Iraqis and foreigners. Yet until very recently virtually everything needed by the workers and their families — food, clothing, and other necessities — was imported. Stores in Kirkuk still stock mostly foreign goods: butter from Australia, fruit preserves from New Zealand, meats and powdered milk from Holland and Denmark, orange juice from Florida. Locally made products are only rarely available. Despite nearby agricultural land and its potential, oil camp purchasing power has not, in two decades, set off a small-scale agricultural revolution leading to food and textile processing industries in northern Iraq.

The same applies to Iran. Here during the three decades prior to 1947 the oil installations were isolated from the rest of the country. Oil workers lived well, but little of what they consumed came from Iran. Iranians and foreigners alike lived lives far removed from the rest of the populace in Khuzistan. To all but a few, plateau Iran meant virtually nothing. And Teheran to most oil workers was an unknown and legendary fleshpot inhabited by absentee landlords and politicians. Few links existed, economic or other.

Yet there has, since World War II, been a change in the situation. Movements for governmental reform in Iraq and Iran began expressing themselves in economic development programs, which needed not only oil earnings for sustenance, but also an entrepreneurial class able to provide more goods and services. Fervid nationalists began increasingly to direct epithets at oil companies, not merely because they had made contracts with "corrupt" governments but because they had not set out actively to use wage bills and local purchasing as tools for development. Two little, rather than too much, "imperialism" vexed these citizens. By 1950 oil companies themselves had accumulated enough experience with local development programs, in Venezuela in particular, to conclude that these might check, or at least slow down, nationalization movements such as beset them in Mexico. Finally, the shut-down at Abadan galvanized the oil industry into self-appraisal and a search for operating practices which would permit continued existence.

The so-called "integration" programs resulted. Since 1950

these have become increasingly important aspects of the relation between oil companies and Middle Eastern governments and people. Broadly speaking, "integration" has come to mean a concerted effort by companies to encourage growth of local enterprise through studied use of local contractors and suppliers for company jobs, to promote expenditure of employee wages for locally made goods, to afford employees a chance to become home owners, in short to make oil operations "one" enterprise rather than "the" enterprise in Middle Eastern countries.[1]

Integration (without use of the term) actually began in Saudi Arabia during World War II, when shortages of American personnel caused the Arabian American Oil Company to subcontract projects to local entrepreneurs better able to collect necessary workers. Under the arrangement, Aramco let contracts to Lebanese firms and itself oversaw construction. Satisfied with results, the company continued the practice after the war but varied procedures by hiring two contractors for each job — one local, to hire workers and do the job, another usually British or American, to supervise and inspect the project.

The same arrangement was employed by Aramco's parent companies when they built the trans-Arabian pipeline from the Persian Gulf to the Mediterranean. Local contractors employed more than 7000 workers for the task. By the time Tapline was completed and operating, in 1949, Aramco itself had created its Arab Development Division, more recently titled the Arab Industrial Development Department (AID), and was trying actively to encourage local businesses associated with the oil industry in Saudi Arabia.

Since 1950 the AID has provided loans, encouragement, and technical assistance to Saudi merchants and contractors and has helped them to establish, in the Al Hasa province towns near the oil camps, ice factories, electric power companies, bottling works, transportation firms, and countless other ventures. The aim of AID has been to employ Aramco's collective technical skills, company requirements, and employee wage bills as a stimulus to economic development generally, and to strengthen its host nation's economic collateral circulation.

Integration figures for Saudi Arabia are illustrative. By late 1957 Aramco was renting more than 600 vehicles from Saudi firms (25 per cent more than it had rented in 1956) and was hiring a constantly growing list of items such as air compressors, welding machines, automobiles. Its AID efforts had created dozens of new firms; surveys of Dammam and Al Khobar divulged that nine tenths of the 1100 firms now operating in these communities began less than a decade ago, three quarters less than four years ago, and forty per cent within the past year. In all, Aramco paid more than $10 million during 1957 to local contractors of various sorts and bought goods worth just over $1 million through Saudi suppliers.

Aramco has also undertaken to purchase food products in Lebanon and since 1950 has steadily increased the volume of Lebanese-grown apples, oranges, meats, and vegetables of all kinds shipped to Saudi Arabia. Faced initially with the usual uncertainties over quality, packing, and time of delivery, Aramco came gradually to operate a small-scale technical assistance program for suppliers in Beirut. This led to the singling out of a dozen businessmen able to deliver proper quantities and qualities of produce ordered, at agreed-upon prices. Invariably these merchants invested in Western-made processing equipment and erected establishments much more modern than those of their competitors.

By the end of 1957 Aramco was buying goods worth just under $2 million yearly through Beirut and was paying over $750,000 yearly to Lebanese-owned airlines to transport the produce on nightly flights to Dhahran. In the five-year period of operation its program gave notable stimulus to systematic techniques of production and market-handling for fruits and vegetables from Lebanon. At least one new Lebanese-owned and -operated airline began, and several others made substantial profits from the business.

Aramco has also, in recent years, promoted a home-ownership scheme for its local employees. Endeavoring to promote "natural" communities (preferred by Arab employees to walled "company" towns), Aramco has advanced loans, helped in planning, and installed public utilities from settlements near Dhahran, Abqaiq, and Ras Tanura. By late 1957 almost 700 homes had been built and moved into under these auspices, approximately half of them in that year.

Integration in Iraq began later, in 1952. There, in the south of the country, the Basrah Petroleum Company, an affiliate of the Iraq Petroleum Company, found itself with new fields to operate, burgeoning production, growing payrolls, and no established pattern of supply procedure or tradition to break. Under L. J. Teyssot, the company's general manager, BPC launched an integration venture which has subsequently become a much discussed prototype for similar projects throughout the Middle East.

Teyssot's scheme consisted of such innovations as the following: placing the company's head offices in rented quarters in the center of the Ashar district in Basrah (rather than building a walled camp away from town); consistently widening the range of company needs purchased locally — particularly those which could be manufactured rather than imported; directing that foreign employees live in rented houses throughout Basrah town rather than in company bungalows; consciously turning over to Iraqi subcontractors a growing number of engineering and transportation tasks; developing a home ownership scheme which served the dual function of permitting employees to acquire property while local contractors got the construction business; serving as cosponsor of an annual industries fair in Basrah; helping Basrah Liwa authorities to cope with the problems (related to water, sewage, schools, and the rest) caused by growing company payrolls. In the latter instance, the company consciously tried to strengthen the local institutions running public utilities and education rather than choosing the more efficient alternative of doing the job itself.

By 1957 the BPC integration program had led to the local purchase of company needs totaling just under $500,000 yearly (exclusive of food purchases, which far exceeded this figure), the subcontracting to Iraqi firms of over half the company's construction work, supervision of the erection of more than 100 employee-owned homes yearly, the turning over to local firms of all but a small fraction of the company's transport requirements. In the process BPC came to deal regularly with more than 300 local entrepreneurs.

In northern Iraq integration took a slower and much less dramatic tack. There the Iraq and Mosul Petroleum Companies have extended local purchasing and subcontracting where possible — a difficult task when operations are long established and foreign suppliers of goods firmly entrenched. From a microscopic figure prior to 1953, local contract payments increased tenfold during the next three years, and transport contracts doubled in volume in one year, 1955–56. By 1957 the Mosul Petroleum Company was purchasing almost 23 per cent of its needs through local suppliers and merchants.

The most significant feature of integration in northern

Iraq has been the IPC home ownership scheme. Begun in 1950 after several years of study, the undertaking set out originally to build 150 houses a year for sale to Iraqi employees through 12–20 year loans at 4½ per cent interest. The initial capital was provided by an Iraqi Bank, the oil company absorbed administrative and management expense and responsibility, and Iraqi contractors bid on the projects. By careful study of costs and inspection of building material, contractors' profits were limited to 10 per cent. The limitation represented a calculated effort to encourage Kirkuk entrepreneurs and to discourage influx of Baghdad contractors, whose appetites for profits purportedly exceeded the relatively modest 10 per cent.

The IPC home ownership scheme works roughly as follows. An employee interested in home purchase applies to the company for approval of a loan application, in the course of which he selects a housing plan ranging in cost from about $3,500 to $15,000. (The "average" house selected so far costs about $5,000.) If he is recommended by his manager, if he has several years of satisfactory service, and if he can pass a perfunctory physical examination, he gets a loan. To qualify financially, he is supposed to advance 10 per cent of the loan total, but since few employees have savings of this magnitude, the company customarily makes funds available by subtracting the amount from the employee's expected terminal pay. The company provides land and retains title to property until amortization is completed. As payment goes on, the employee carries an insurance policy designed to provide his family clear title should he die.

By the end of 1957, 600 IPC workers, out of a labor force of roughly 4000, had moved into houses constructed on these terms. In the process, a dozen locally owned and operated contracting businesses evolved, all constructing homes according to the plans and plot-sites required by the oil company and its Iraqi bankers.

After 1954 integration in Iraq and Saudi Arabia served as prototypes for similar efforts in Iran. Before the Abadan troubles the Anglo Iranian Oil Company had done little to insert itself into the economy of Iran, and indeed, in the opinion of many experts, could do little. The international Consortium arrangement, however, committed participating companies and the Iranian Government to a plan of integration.

This so far has taken the form of extraordinary increases in local purchasing by operating companies in Iran. From an insignificant pre-1950 figure, Consortium affiliates upped local ordering to $10 million in 1956 and over $12 million in 1957 — between 15 and 20 per cent of total purchases. In addition the Consortium has set out actively to study means of encouraging production, by Iranian entrepreneurs, of goods and services designed to satisfy demand from the country's 65,000 oil workers. And local construction contracts (admittedly small in view of the long established nature of Iran's oil installations) are awarded with preference to Iranian entrepreneurs.

In Kuwait geography so far has prevented development of anything resembling a "natural" economy. Forced initially to buy virtually everything abroad, the Kuwait Oil Company has since 1954 adopted the practice of placing orders for imported goods through Kuwaiti merchants. And all but the most technically complicated construction projects are handled through contracts with local businessmen. The company has also encouraged construction of ice plants, bottling works, and other locally managed enterprises designed to service KOC's labor force.

Integration therefore has become common practice in the Middle East today and has gone on long enough to permit tentative evaluation of the effort and a clearer statement of the dimensions of the problem. The following conclusions may be drawn.

It must first be recognized that integration still plays a very minor quantitative role in the overall economy of the Middle East. Companies purchase about 10 per cent of their needs locally, and despite their good intentions it seems doubtful, in view of the industry's high-level technology and dependence on Western suppliers for complicated equipment, that this figure can be increased greatly. That 10 per cent which is bought locally, moreover, still consists largely of orders placed through Arab or Iranian merchants for Western imported goods. The amount of goods actually made locally is still very small indeed.

Integration's great successes to date, moreover, have been in the field of contracting. Here Middle Eastern counterparts of the Western "producing" entrepreneur (as contrasted with the bazaar merchant) have developed and in the process are creating jobs and performing an educational function while building tank farms, pipelines, and roads. The three partners in the highly successful Lebanese Contracting and Trading Company, all former employees of the Iraq Petroleum Company, epitomize the evolution of this type of business leader. But the fact remains that the construction business in the area still gains its basic sustenance, directly or indirectly, from the oil industry. The significance of contracting to area-wide economic growth should not be overestimated.

Nor have home-ownership schemes yet turned the majority of oil workers into property-owning freeholders. By the end of 1957, less than 2000 homes had been built for employee ownership — 600 each in Kirkuk and Arabia, and several hundred elsewhere. Out of an area-wide local labor force of over 100,000 workers, homeowners still represent a small minority.

The integration programs definitely provide a vehicle for

education and broadening of the area's technological base. Oil companies have proved most sympathetic to resignations by local employees embarking on businesses of their own and in some instances have promoted these businesses through contracts. Several dozen contracting firms, at least one locally owned and managed airline, at least one highly efficient research and translation agency, and dozens of merchant-suppliers have spun off from oil companies in this fashion. Companies have come increasingly to regard such shifts of employment as transfers of investment rather than loss of skilled employees. The companies' role in business education is substantial.

In this same category, the growing tendency of local contractors to form partnerships with Western engineering companies — partially an outgrowth of the supervising-company arrangements earlier favored by oil companies — has definitely led to improved technology and has permitted local firms to add steadily to the range of complex jobs they can not only bid on but actually do. A decade ago, for a local firm to attempt construction of a bridge across the Euphrates at Baghdad would have been unthinkable. Recently one local firm did the job handily, and a dozen others could have done as well. A growing number of Middle East contractors now maintain active working relations with foreign firms.

Integration, furthermore, has proved most successful in those communities relatively well endowed with a combination of natural resources and a sophisticated society. Basrah, with a long history of contact with the outside world, and located in an area where settled agriculture had long flourished, offered a receptive milieu to an oil company intent on integrating itself. Kirkuk, an isolated community even today, has proved understandably resistant. How far integration can go in Saudi Arabia and Kuwait, where hostile physical environments and problems of public administration and denomadization join, is questionable. In these communities, initial statistical successes prove little.

Really successful economic integration is still hindered by the geographical and cultural isolation common in the Middle East. The separation between Khuzistan and plateau Iran has already been mentioned. Aramco operates, for integration purposes, almost entirely in the eastern province of Saudi Arabia. The Nejd, which contains the country's capital and its second center of population, lies an eight hour train ride away. The Red Sea communities of the Hejaz lie still farther westward. They too, like Al Hasa, are separated from Riyadh by a murderously hot and forbidding desert. Integration activities are still largely local in scope.

Integration's effect on savings habits and internal private investment in the Middle East so far defies accurate calculation. Unquestionably most of the estimated $10 million of private investment which now goes into the eastern province of Arabia is directly traceable to integration. Yet how much of this money has been weaned away from earlier investment in luxury apartments in Cairo, Beirut, or Damascus is still anybody's guess. Iranian private investment in Khuzistan is obviously aimed toward profits from integration. So too is private capital now flowing into lathes, construction equipment, trucks, and other producers' goods in the oil communities in Iraq. But to assess magnitudes or cumulative effects with accuracy is impossible.

It is also too early to judge the political and social implications of integration. Nobody knows whether the Pygmalion-Galatea relationship of oil company and local entrepreneur will make the latter into a Middle Eastern counterpart of the British wool merchants of the seventeenth and eighteenth centuries, whose effect on the politics as well as the economy of England was tremendous. Nor can one judge the cumulative effect of the importation — indirectly traceable to integration — of non-Western minorities. The Goans, Pakistanis, Palestinians, Lebanese, and Syrians bring with them not only technical skills but frequently, it is said, exotic political ideas. Can integration be a tool to blunt the ire of the Middle East's "angry young men" who link oil companies with exploitation of the people by so-called feudal rulers?

Oil companies meanwhile can do little but proceed with integration at full throttle. Thoughtful executives recognize both the economic limits of the undertaking and its political uncertainties. Creation of what the London *Economist* terms a "sense of common interest" between themselves and Middle Easterners has become to them a carefully calculated and well intentioned risk.[2] For them to take advice from the critics of integration — one of whom has described the policies as a "telling illustration of the decline of the West" — now seems impossible, and in the mid-twentieth century inadvisable.[3] But integration is still very much a gambler's throw.

# VII

## Economic Planning in the Middle East

Economic planning is a growing feature of the Middle Eastern landscape.[1] As in the West, the process serves as subject for constant debate. Arguments differ little from those advanced by proponents and opponents of planning in the United States or Europe, and Middle Eastern policy makers face the same terrifying decisions as their Western confreres.

The planners, unquestionably a growing majority, urge international collaboration to promote economic growth by measures more drastic and rapid than are permitted by traditional private trade and capital transfers. They express steadily weakening faith in the price system as an allocator of resource. For them, "balanced growth" has become an attainable and desired goal. Government should expand its role.

Allied against the planners, oddly enough, are strange bedfellows, economists representing the two poles of extreme conservatism and Marxian liberalism. The conservatives see planning boards in Asia as a great Trojan Horse towing the barbarous contrivances of post-1900 Western economics into countries hitherto innocent of deficit finance, progressive taxation, and the like. The Marxists are equally opposed. One of them puts their case as follows: "The injection of [capitalist economic] planning into a

society living in the twilight between feudalism and Capitalism cannot but result in additional corruption, larger
and more artful evasions of the law and more brazen abuses
of authority." [2]

The first attempt at economic planning in the Middle
East was Ataturk's five-year plans during the 1930's. A
vague mixture of contemporary German and Russian planning, Turkey's plans consisted mainly of public investments in heavy industry. The insertion of the Karabuk steel
mill, an aircraft engine factory, and a rayon spinning mill
into an Anatolian peasant society proved abrasive indeed.
In a country with primitive public administration, short
on entrepreneurs, lacking private savings for investment,
without a highway grid, the plants meant little. Ataturk's
schemes were in no sense integrated programs of investment. As symbols of national strength, they probably contributed to Ataturk's designs, but they were hardly successes in economic terms.

Iran before 1950 provided a slightly different example.
The Millspaugh Missions of the 1920's and 1940's gave Iran
a series of advisers, many of whom were extremely able.
Lacking a mandate to produce and operate an integrated
plan, the advisers worked to rationalize Iranian government practices, to improve record keeping, tax collection,
and monetary issue practices. They probably helped spend
Iran's oil revenues more effectively. But regardless, the
country lacked private investment capital, ordinary government budgets sopped up most of the country's oil income,
and, as in Turkey, human resources and lack of social overhead improvements joined to check effectively any measur-
able advance in Iran's net per capita income. One benefit
accruing from the Missions was the exposure, one of the
first, provided its American advisers to the complexities
of economic development in the Middle East.

Another exposure came to Overseas Consultants Incorporated, a post-World War II undertaking imbued with a Pilgrim Father sort of combination of secular missionary zeal and desire for financial gain. Iran after the war had much more money than before — left there by Allied armies. But it had little else. OCI shaped a plan for Iran which was on the whole reasonable and which outlined massive improvements in the country's highways, communications, public health, and education. Its efforts stalled before the merciless efficiency with which Iranian government bureaucracy disposed of oil income, which was admittedly too small for large-scale investments, while permitting virtually no constructive expenditure. Before it withdrew in 1949, OCI shaped the first rough framework for a serviceable economic development plan in the Middle East.

The ten year plan launched in 1946 by the Crown Colony Secretariat on Cyprus called for total public outlays of about $30 million. Financed entirely from government sources, the scheme made little effort to relate expenditure or projects in one sector to those in others. Nor did it set out to stimulate or channel private investment, domestic and foreign, on the island. The plan's basic accomplishment was to invest a portion of Cyprus' expanded revenues, from copper exports and military installations, in an excellent highway system and power grid, malaria eradication, improved water supply, better education, and other social overhead improvements. It virtually ignored the island's private sector. Nor did it really attack Cyprus' pressing rural problems.

Pre-1950 economic planning in the Middle East was, in a sentence, essentially a governmental affair and had as its major accomplishment a circulation of awareness of the magnitude of the problem. What has been called "conspicuous industrialization" in prewar Turkey, monumental studies and unheeded (and sometimes useless) advice by Westerners to Iran, and the basically useful program in Cyprus accented the need for more funds for investment, improved management and public administration to utilize such funds, and, most important, a change in the very fabric of Middle Eastern society if economic growth was to quicken.

In 1950 all this began to change, breathtakingly. Reasons are well known: the 50–50 oil profit arrangement and soaring production which made astronomical sums available for public investment within a few years; the snowballing momentum of the United States Foreign Aid program, which by 1950 was pushing up Europe's demand for Middle East oil while pumping $200 million yearly into Turkey, slightly less into Iran, $40 million into Israel, and smaller amounts into the Arab countries; Israel's consolidation and massive fund-raising venture which has transferred $200–$300 million yearly from the West to its economy; a private investment boom in Lebanon and Syria, due largely to the Korean War, influx of Arab refugees from Israel, and expenditures by oil-rich shaikhs from the Persian Gulf and Arabia; soaring copper production and prices in Cyprus, coupled with the island's growing importance to Britain's military establishment in the eastern Mediterranean; emergence in several countries of cabinet ministers and civil servants intent on promoting economic planning.

Among Islamic countries, Iraq was the first to enunciate a comprehensive development plan. Owning just about everything its neighbors lack — water, land, a favorable land-man ratio, geographic isolation, willingness to employ (and heed) the advice of foreign technical experts, a law earmarking 70 per cent of oil revenues for development — Iraq set out in 1951 to re-establish an infrastructure which had undergone erosion since Roman times. In that year the Development Board got about $20 million, $5 per Iraqi, for investment. By 1956 the board's annual income had reached $170 million, $35 per citizen. During 1958 the board aimed to spend almost $280 million, more than $50 per Iraqi.

To date Iraq's schemes have been, with minor exceptions, completely financed from public funds, and investment has gone chiefly into land and water improvements — dams and barrages, reduction of salt and moisture in the soil, depressions and reservoirs such as Wadi Thartar and Habbaniya for flood control and conservation. Substantial investment has also gone into transport — railroad, highway, airline, and port facilities. In recent years large sums have begun to flow into education (Iraq doubled its primary and secondary school student body between 1951 and 1956) and low-cost public housing.

As adventures in planning, Iraq's projects represent essentially attempts to overtake more developed countries by massive social overhead investments. To date the Development Board has shown little interest in the private investor, the assumption being that he will at the proper time mount the vehicle of economic growth set in motion from programs in soil improvement, education, and transportation. Nor did the board, prior to the overthrow of the monarchy in July 1958, attempt comprehensive land-reform measures. Despite stifling overconcentration of ownership (mostly in the hands of shaikhs and landowners who made up Iraq's parliaments), the Development Board, for political reasons, skirted the issue through investments in projects such as Dujaila and Diwaniya — resettlement schemes using reclaimed government lands. The board's policy was, before late 1958, to avoid head-on collision with Iraq's landowning parliament while embracing the hope that success in re-

settlement would convince the shaikhs that smaller holdings, producing more per unit of land, were in their good
interests as well as those of Iraq's peasants.

The Iraq plan, therefore, has consisted of a vast wager,
by public investments, on its people's willingness to move
themselves from the abject squalor of the environs of
Baghdad and Basrah and the southern marshes and northern
hill country into conditions of greater affluence, material
and cultural. Despite its admirable features and accomplishments (for the first time in recorded history, for example, the civilization-destroying yearly floods of the Tigris
and Euphrates rivers can now be checked and the waters
used for perennial irrigation), the plan is not yet an integrated one and only partially mobilizes the nation's human
resources.

More comprehensive is the five year plan currently being
set in motion by Pakistan. Drafted after three years of study
by the Pakistan Planning Board (aided by foreign advisers
headed by Professor Edward Mason of Harvard), the plan
attempts to correlate investment within and between the
public and private sectors of the economy. Essentially conservative, it blueprints a set of investment directions and
magnitudes totaling $2½ billion over five years — about
$7 yearly per Pakistani. According to the plan's schedules,
about four fifths of investment will be public money and
one fifth private. Foreign exchange components will nec-
essarily be high, and foreign aid averaging over $100 million
yearly is envisaged. By a series of measures, direct (such as
the Pakistan Industrial Development Corporation, a quasi-
governmental undertaking) and indirect (tax relief, access
to foreign exchange, and so on), the plan aims to enlist
Pakistani businessmen, as well as foreign firms and investors,
in the growth process.

Clearly the most comprehensive plan yet written for an

Islamic country, the Pakistan scheme at this juncture is just that, a plan. The problems it faces are gigantic — eighty million citizens separated culturally and geographically by the Indian subcontinent, excessive dependence on "problem crops" (wheat and cotton) for sustenance, a history of paralyzing crop failure and floods with dreary regularity in both East and West Pakistan, need for large amounts of foreign aid to weight the balance of investment, the standard Islamic land tenure pattern of overconcentration combined with overfragmentation, to mention only a few. Put into effect piecemeal since 1956, the plan has as yet had few discernible results. As a blueprint for development it has achieved general acclaim.

Iran likewise is attempting erection of a comprehensive development plan. The Seven Year Plan Organization has begun to overhaul and revise the original framework suggested by Overseas Consultants Incorporated, aiming to employ funds now earmarked by law for development from oil earnings. Already the plan organization's legal share of revenues exceeds $100 million yearly. Assisted, like Pakistan and Iraq, by foreign advisers, Iran is moving toward a strengthened and more integrated plan.

Two problems particularly vex Iran's planners. First is the constant pressure for more funds from those who direct the country's ordinary government budget. As development proceeds, demands on the normal government services increase. The Iranian civil service has not yet lost its skill in the art of absorbing oil revenues. Under pressure from many interested groups, the Iranian Majlis, for example, recently passed a law, corollary to the economic development decree, which permits the country's ordinary budget to acquire more than its 30 per cent share of Iran's annual oil earnings, provided the Seven Year Plan Organization can borrow an equivalent amount abroad. Subject to such pressure during 1958, the Plan Organization sought more than $80 million abroad. At this rate Iran's aggregate foreign debt could shortly approach $500 million. The competition between funds for development and those to run the government continues meanwhile with unabated intensity.

Another problem is internal isolation, geographical and cultural, within Iran. Oil operations in lowland Khuzistan, about which widespread external economies might well develop, are far removed from the life of plateau Iran. So, too, are Iranians who stand to participate in those external economies, as suppliers of goods and services to the oil company and its workers. To attack the problem Iran has sublet part of the development task in Khuzistan to an American firm, the Development and Resources Corporation. A TVA-like regional planning effort is under way, involving dams, factories, and the like, but definitive attachment of Khuzistan to plateau Iran is still a major hurdle. Iran is also launching a smaller-scale, Khuzistan-like scheme in Kerman, also with American private advisers.

Israel presents still a different case. Although it is sponsoring a seven year plan, Israel's extraordinary economic advance to date has been directed by decentralized arrangements. But it *has* been directed. More than a dozen agencies — government ministries and bureaus, Histadrut, productivity institutes — have each evolved elaborate plans for their particular operations. Investment decisions derive from a blending of social philosophy and economic profitability, with the former element more dominant than elsewhere in the Middle East. At this juncture, Israel offers a mosaic of plans rather than a coordinated whole, with public or quasi-public agencies definitely in command.

Still another variation is provided by Kuwait. While leading ascetic personal lives (by Middle Eastern ruling-class standards), the ruler and his advisers have tried systematically to invest the tiny shaikhdom's soaring income constructively. Beginning with little more than money — Kuwait has no natural fresh water, no settled agriculture worth mentioning, no tradition of industry or international trade, and only 250,000 citizens — Shaikh Abdullah el-Salem el-Sabbah created a planning board and put vast sums into housing, hospitals, schools, water distillation plants, town improvements, and the usual public utilities. Quickly hitting the limits of his country's capital absorptive capacity, the Shaikh undertook concomitantly, after 1950, to invest his unused revenues in British Treasury Certificates. In 1958, for example, the Shaikhdom's budget, including investments in development, was estimated at over $250 million (more than $1000 per Kuwaiti), and funds entering the London money market (which today is said to count the Shaikh its biggest single provider of capital) will reportedly total just under $100 million.

Kuwait operates essentially without a plan. Its expenditures are based on decisions by the Shaikh, advised by a planning board headed by one of his heirs presumptive. Investment depends on the ruler's conclusions as to the Shaikhdom's level of earnings for the year, how much money can be spent effectively (and on what), how much should be invested abroad. His country presents a picture of *ad hoc* economic planning under conditions of tribal rule with a sovereign intent on improving his subjects' lot. Kuwaitis are infinitely better housed, clothed, fed, and transported than ever before. School children attend marvelously equipped free schools, receive liberal pocket-money, free lunches, and instruction from Egyptian, Lebanese, and Palestinian teachers. As an experiment in social welfare improvement, Kuwait is remarkable. As an example of prospective indigestion from too much capital, it is disquieting indeed.

Saudi Arabia, until very recently, has likewise spent its

oil revenues without reference to a plan. Like Kuwait, Saudi Arabia's tribal monarchy is absolute. And like Iran, the kingdom consists of several separate, and widely isolated, entities — the Eastern Province of Al Hasa, the central Nejd, and the Red Sea province of Hejaz. Investments over the past decade by the Crown have gone into ports in Jeddah and the Eastern Province, a railroad from Dammam to Riyadh, a magnificent set of ministries in Riyadh, a processing center for Mecca-bound Moslem pilgrims in Jeddah, hospitals and schools. No coordination of investments has taken place, and the volume of constructive investment, compared to the kingdom's oil earnings, has been tiny.

Only recently, since mid-1958, has Saudi Arabia attempted to rationalize its public finance and expenditures of oil income, by strengthening the Saudi Arabian monetary agency, declaring a moratorium on the import of foreign automobiles, and revising its governing arrangement to permit enforcement of a program of economic austerity. The monetary agency currently (since 3 June 1958) controls all foreign exchange transfers, directs a fund to stabilize open market fluctuations of the Saudi rial, and has authority to devote budget surpluses to increasing gold backing of the currency — profligacy of the past decade having cut the gold cover to 25 per cent. Monetary measures alone so far distinguish public economic planning in Saudi Arabia.

Planning of a different sort, without use of the term, has gone on in the eastern province under auspices of the Arabian American Oil Company. Anxious to divest itself of the myriad of service functions unrelated to the petroleum industry it now performs, Aramco has outlined a comprehensive set of practicable small-industry investments. Admittedly dependent on the oil company at this juncture, investments in small-scale industry might well,

Aramco estimates, total $15–$18 million yearly within the next five years.

Syria has also turned only recently to economic planning. Enjoying a private investment boom during its first ten years, Syria from 1945 to 1955 advanced rapidly, as it opened its Jezira to cotton and wheat growing, expanded its industrial production with wartime savings, and, through the stimulus of Korean War shortages, created the funds to erect vast warrens of luxury apartments in the environs of Aleppo and Damascus. By 1955 the boom had begun to run down, and in that year Syria enunciated its first seven year plan.[3]

Drawn up by Syrians, with little direct help from foreigners, the Syrian seven year plan reflected nevertheless the influence of two earlier surveys by Western advisers — the first a study by a private British firm, completed in 1948, and the second a study by the International Bank for Reconstruction and Development, published in 1955. Both urged public works investments designed to improve Syria's water supplies, soil, harbors, and transportation, most of which the private boom had proved inadequate. The Syrian plan of 1955 followed this theme, albeit more modestly than the bank's experts recommended, and called for seven-year outlays of just under $200 million. Funds should come from taxation, oil-transit earnings, bond sales, foreign loans, and inflationary finance.

In late 1957 Syria added to its seven year plan by signing a supplementary aid agreement with the Soviet Union. Under this the planned levels of investment more than doubled, to a total of about $400 million — nearer to the levels recommended by the IBRD mission and within the same general framework of expenditure. Russia agreed in the contract to provide Syria with technical assistance for project surveys *and* implementation, and loan funds to carry them out — all at 2½ per cent interest. The Soviet Union agreed, in short, in a studiously vague document, to take up the IBRD and Syrian government plans virtually intact and assist in their implementation. Should investment go on as scheduled, public funds amounting to about $100 per Syrian will be invested in the nation's social overhead during the plan period.

The remaining countries of the Middle East — Turkey, Egypt, Lebanon, and Jordan — have so far practiced little that might be termed planning. Lacking oil, none has faced the need to dispose of swollen government incomes. All have development boards of sorts, but the influence of these on regular government bureaus, which retain control of tax revenues and foreign aid funds, is far less than is the case in Iraq and Iran. Turkey, moreover, in a postwar re-action against Ataturk's Etatism, has come to symbolize a form of economic freedom deemed chaotic by many observers. Lebanon, too, is held up frequently as one of the world's few remaining citadels of truly laissez-faire capitalism.

Interpretation of the evidence permits several broad conclusions regarding economic planning in the Middle East as so far tried. Initially, one quickly reaches the conclusion that planning today is still very much a national and not a regional matter. The many international schemes for the Jordan valley, well intentioned and technically feasible, have so far foundered on the shoal of the utter inability of Arabs and Israelis to come to terms. Little too has come of the myriad proposals for inter-Arab cooperation, most of which have as their central theme investment of Kuwait's excess revenues in Arab countries with more absorptive capacity. Unless a miracle occurs, planning will continue to evolve within nation states in the Middle East, not between them.

Next, economic planning as currently practiced in the Middle East is very much an unproved entity. The successes (in pure economic terms) of those states which have tried to coordinate investment have undeniably been great. Iraq, Israel, Cyprus, and Kuwait have all gone ahead strikingly. Yet none of the "planning" states has approached the point where dependence on the outside world seems lessening, or where a take-off into sustained growth appears imminent. Cyprus remains a ward of the West. Israel estimates that, despite its achievements since 1947, it will require $250 million yearly for at least another seven years, probably much longer, to offset its trade deficits. Except for oil, Kuwait clearly lacks the natural resources to broaden its economic base and attain even minimal internal self-sufficiency. Iraq so far has only begun to mobilize its entire population, and its statistical advance is largely attributable to increased oil earnings, only secondarily to increased expansion throughout its economy. Iran and Pakistan, now enunciating plans, still have extremely low per capita incomes and cannot yet point to measurable increase in real terms.

Alongside the "planning" states are examples of countries which have registered substantial growth despite a virtual absence of coordinated investment. Syria, Lebanon, and Turkey have all gone ahead at 3 to 7 per cent per capita yearly, pushed on by high levels of private investment. While the booms obviously have run down in all three countries, they accent the role playable by a sophisticated business community, for a time at least, under conditions of relative laissez faire in the Middle East.

It now seems evident, however, even in the citadels of laissez faire, that public investments will outweigh private outlays during the next decade. In Iraq, Iran, Kuwait, Saudi Arabia, Egypt, Jordan, and Israel the balance is already on the public side, with more than 60 per cent of net investment being conducted under government auspices. Syria and Lebanon, for the first time, seem intent on reversing their ratios, which have for a decade been approximately 80 per cent private and 20 per cent public, and ploughing large public funds (to be obtained by Syria from Russian loans and by Lebanon from United States foreign aid) into social overhead improvements. Even Turkey, reportedly at United States instigation, is contemplating more co-ordination of its investment, public and private. This will probably mean a rise in public outlays.

Despite the increase in volume of public investment, the Middle East remains, on the basis of public expenditures as per cent of gross national product, more "capitalist" than most Western industrial nations. France, Britain, Sweden and the United States, for example, all spend more than 20 per cent of their gross national product through public channels.[4] Most of the Middle East (Turkey, Egypt, Iran, Lebanon, and Syria, which together contain about seventy million people) still spends less than 20 per cent of national income under public auspices. Israel, Iraq, Kuwait, and Saudi Arabia, having swollen outside incomes payable directly to government, spend nearer to 50 per cent of national income publicly. But they contain only about thirteen million people, and despite oil revenues and gifts from abroad, their national incomes total much less than those of their more populous neighbors. While on this basis slightly more "socialist" than India (which spends less than 9 per cent of national income through its government), the Middle East today is, then, despite its plans, in some ways more "capitalist" than the industrial West it strives to overtake.

Government action on land reform further illustrates the essentially conservative outlook of Middle East economic planning today. The land reform programs of Egypt, Syria, Iraq, Turkey, and Pakistan very definitely permit retention of holdings large enough to qualify their owners for the title of wealthy men. Two hundred acres of Nile delta land, the top limit per owner under Egypt's land reform law of 1952, was at the time worth almost $500,000. Irrigated lands in the Syrian Jezira, the Punjab in Pakistan, the Chukorova plain in Turkey, or Southern Iran, while not as valuable as the soil of Egypt, reach high values per 200 acres. The land reform programs seem destined to redistribute income more drastically than wealth. And future historians might well label them conservative undertakings indeed.

The same label cannot, however, be applied to Syria's economic agreements with the Soviet Union and Egypt. Adhering to date to expenditures outlined by Western advisers from the IBRD, Syria has only recently begun to increase the flow of public investment funds. Its agreement with Russia calls for loans and advisers only, and avoids reference to Syrian policy toward economic development. The Syrian budget for 1958–59 represents little change from preceding documents, except for an increase in defense funds. The arrangement will offer a test run on the extent to which Soviet advisers can influence the economic philosophy of a Middle Eastern nation.

Russia by her entry into economic planning in the Middle East may well help to shoulder a burden which the West so far has tried to carry single-handed. Except in Syria, economic planning in the area has been essentially a Western affair, with Western advisers and economic philosophy dominant. The West has been blamed for failures of the process. Now that the Soviet Union has abandoned its essentially negative approach and has itself ventured onto the shaky limb of promoting economic development in a highly sensitive and often difficult Middle Eastern nation, some spreading of the awesome risks seems inevitable. The West might gain from the process.

Attempts at economic planning have, moreover, regardless of their success or failure in quantitative economic terms, played an undeniably constructive role in acquainting more Middle Easterners with the basic facts of their national economies. Planning boards and "plans" inevitably lead to promotion of studies and inventories of national resource and income, foreign exchange reserves and requirements, and the other ingredients which make for intelligent investment decisions, public and private. The residual effect should be fewer dams built before there are collateral facilities to utilize the water, fewer factories built too large for local demand, fewer of the other extravagances common to Western economic history but too expensive for a developing Middle East.

Yet the Middle East planners obviously need also to make certain that occasional "extravagances" with creative and unforeseen ends can indeed occur. In Israel, for example, the widespread use of planning has, in the opinion of some, discouraged broad-spectrum investments by private businessmen — many of which would fail but an occasional one of which, contrary to rational predictions, might well become a leading industry with widespread cumulative effect. As Professor Abba Lerner has said of Israel, the Islamic Middle East also needs to learn "when to plan *not* to plan" [5] as badly as it needs to avoid the waste of laissez faire mixed with Oriental atavism.

Finally, the plans certainly will offer an admirable laboratory in which the refinements of Western economic thought and analysis may be checked for relevancy. Graduated income taxes, purchase taxes, inflationary financing of development, input-output tables and accounting as measuring rods for investment success and X-rays for the economy's structure, to mention a few — all are increasingly on trial. Western economists cannot but learn much, regardless of the outcome.

It is reasonable to assume, therefore, that economic planning will increase markedly in the Middle East over the next decade. Most Western economists will endorse the process despite feelings of uneasiness over the eventual outcome. A reasonable forecast is for continued growth of public funds for investment from oil earnings, United States aid, gifts by international Jewry, German reparations, and military base expenditures. So long as this continues, and until and unless (as seems highly unlikely) private investment funds come forward to challenge these, the plans seem imperative. Sadly for the antiplanners, the advice given ten years ago to one Middle Eastern country by a distinguished European economist is no longer heeded. In prescribing for the economy of Lebanon, in 1949, he reportedly said, "I don't know what makes it work. But it seems to do pretty well. I suggest therefore that you leave it alone." [6]

# VIII

## What Can the West Offer?

### 1. ECONOMIC DOCTRINE

What exactly can the West offer the Middle East in the final quarters of the twentieth century? Literature devoted to the West's role in Asia, and including the Middle East in its generalizations, grows daily. It also grows more dismal. The thoughtful American, Englishman, or Frenchman finds it hard to draw cheer from what he reads. The arguments seem to draw intellectual sustenance from Mark Twain's eternal verity that "God looks after drunks, children, and the United States of America."

Much of the self-examination is overdone, some of it is vicious. It is in many respects comparable to the inward-looking criticism of the American literary tradition of 1910–1930.[1] American writers dwell on the mishaps of American land-grant college professors prescribing complicated machines for Iranian farmers with neither the skill to run them nor the income to pay for them. Everybody derides the ill-prepared lingerie tycoons or party-giving heiresses appointed to ambassadorships by Democratic or Republican party patronage. British and French authors, comfortably forgetful of the dismal messes made abroad by their own governments and people — in Abadan, Algeria, and Cyprus, for example — have joined the pack with a set of clinical observations on the mishaps of Americans teetering on the brink of disaster in Asia.[2]

Much of the criticism is merited, yet too much of it has been overdone. The West, and particularly the United States of America, does have something of genuine merit to offer Asia and the Middle East. As these last two chapters will seek to demonstrate, the offering consists of economic doctrine, economic policy, and what, for want of a better term, might be called "a point of view."

First let us consider economic doctrine. The theories, postulates, and tools of analysis of Western economics are increasingly on trial abroad, under circumstances quite different from those in the industrial nations whence they came. Several hundred young men from the Middle East each year are exposed in varying intensities to dosages of Western doctrine. They will face in the future, as their peers do today, complicated decisions on taxation, monetary policy, and investment weighting, to mention only a few. Conditions in the Middle East at this very moment place a staggering burden upon Western economic ideas.

My own conclusion on the validity of Western economic concepts, reached during more than a decade of watching Middle Easterners in their economic setting, parallels that of Professor Peter Bauer on the general subject. Basing his observations on the economic behavior of Africans and South Asians, he has written, "I am now convinced of the very wide applicability to underdeveloped countries of the basic methods of approach of economics and of the more elementary conclusions stemming from these. I am thinking especially of the elements of supply and demand analysis and its simpler conclusions, the tendencies of people to seek activities and occupations which yield the highest net advantage within the opportunities open to them, the implications of the concept of complementary and competitive relationships between productive resources, and many others. Some of these propositions are direct corollaries of the limitation of resources, so that their wide applicability to underdeveloped countries is not in question." [3]

We now know enough about the workings of a series of economies in the Middle East to conclude that in the monetized parts at least, Bauer's words bear relevance. Middle Easterners have long since proved themselves as acquisitive as we Westerners, as skillful at calculation of comparative costs and advantages in various fields of investment, and as possessed as we of capitalist inclinations. In its simpler applications, Western doctrine seems distinctly relevant to the Middle East.

But undeniably the doctrines of the West — based as they are on economies increasingly industrialized, entirely monetized, and owning peculiar institutional structures — quickly lose most of their relevance to the Middle East when they move into the more refined realms. A look at several of the gaps is illustrative.

The first major area in which Western economic theory is unable to make itself useful to the underdeveloped Middle East is in the realm of investment weighting. While dwelling on the theme of balanced growth and the failures of the price system as allocator of resources, to date little written in the West comes close to answering the questions which press public decision makers, and to a lesser degree private investors, as they try to decide where to invest, and how much. The need is greatest in the public sphere, where, as has been shown in earlier chapters, upwards of 60 per cent of the area's investment goes on and where returns are calculated in other than financial terms.

Western economists have built, for example, no really adequate guideposts to indicate what percentages of development funds Middle Eastern nations might intelligently invest either in public-health medicine or in curative medicine. Everybody talks glibly of population explosions and the role of healthier workers in adding to production. But nobody has really reduced the endless discussion to the simple terms of exactly how much, and where, investment in public-health medicine will actually increase the ratio of hands working to mouths eating. Meanwhile investment goes on haphazardly.

Western economists have likewise skirted the issue when it comes to suggesting relative weighting between investments in human beings — education at all levels — and in the customary additions to physical assets. Preliminary research in Pakistan and India has concluded, for example, that there are substantial increases in production taking place which are largely consequences of increases in "human capital." These are only in small measure attributable to funds spent on more traditional investment, such as machinery. Introduction of hybrid corn and resultant increases in yield indicate, as David Bell has suggested, that "the training of additional agricultural extension agents might well result in a larger growth in national output and income than any alternative use of resources." [4]

Western economic doctrine — and educational philosophy — has been equally incapable thus far of suggesting weighting within the fields of education in the Middle East. Since 1950 the American University of Beirut has been analyzing its investments in liberal arts and technical education (medicine, engineering, agriculture) without reaching a remotely satisfactory conclusion as to returns obtainable per dollar of investment. Decisions are made, as at American universities at home, by jousts between deans and faculty committees and on the basis of reports on the institution by distinguished educators brought in for studies. (These recommendations usually parallel the consultant's prejudices brought intact from home: engineering deans, for example, want the students taught more physics and mathematics, liberal arts college presidents recommend more humanities courses in the curriculum, professors of education urge more emphasis on teacher training, and so on.) Guideposts on the subject are virtually nonexistent in Western literature in the field, and decisions are still made essentially through response to visceral instincts, or upon urging from a foundation with funds to spend on a particular project.

Western commercial banking theory, also part of allocation doctrine, has likewise shown severe inadequacies. In assessing the World Bank programs of the past decade one cannot but reach sobering conclusions. A recent study suggests that the IBRD's lending policies (which have in the past decade channeled about 63 per cent of the bank's loan funds into electric power and transport facilities and only about 17 per cent into industry) have probably not, because of their direction, had optimum effect in maximizing rates of income growth and distribution. The IBRD Mission Reports have done an inadequate job of outlining statistical bases and systems of social accounting; these have been of real value to the countries studied, yet in some instances they have been built on admittedly faulty knowledge. The major outlines of development programs suggested by Bank Missions have often been vague, ambiguous, and disconnected. The Reports have often been weak in the matter of investment priorities and alternative opportunities and "pay-offs." The Reports have not done enough to point up the problems of price changes and inflationary pressure which accompany almost all development programs. Finally, the Reports fail to outline really effective incentives to private investment. In short one is led to question the relevance of traditional Western commercial banking theory to areas where bold new programs probably are indicated. The IBRD Reports for Turkey, Iraq, Syria, and Jordan illustrate the problem.[5]

Western economic theories on allocation of investment funds have, in short, assumed that the conditions which spawned them in the industrial West will prevail in the Middle East, have overlooked the need for revision of priorities when faced with heavily weighted public expenditures, have avoided the pressing need to redefine the meaning of capital, and have skirted the issue of how to weight accurately investments in human beings and plants and machinery. The Middle East offers an excellent example of doctrinal weakness in this respect.

Nor has Western economic doctrine yet tailored concepts of income distribution which Middle Eastern nations can accept with reasonable assurance that if applied they will promote lasting economic growth. The area meanwhile manifests widely variant attitudes toward income distribution in its public policies. Israel probably has the most equally distributed income in the world. Cyprus also practices strongly progressive taxation. Both have made rapid statistical advances since 1947. But so too have Syria and Iraq, which exhibit widely unequal incomes and tremendous gaps between rich and poor. Lebanon, with less disparity in its income distribution, has advanced rapidly since World War II. So has Turkey, while distributing its income in a fashion somewhere between that of Iraq and that of Lebanon. Few guideposts exist which really tell Middle Eastern governments whether to follow the West's nineteenth century practices — which concentrated most of the savings for investment in relatively few hands — or more modern fiscal techniques.

Concepts defining and suggesting cures for so-called "disguised unemployment" (referring to that part of the rural labor force which could be removed, given present techniques, without decreasing farm production) have also to date proved inconclusive. Joan Robinson's term, meant originally to apply to skilled industrial workers engaged in menial tasks because their factories had closed down, has become widely accepted in the lore of underdeveloped areas. Charles Issawi, for example, concludes that as much as half the Egyptian peasant labor force is essentially redundant.[6] World Bank studies, more reserved than Issawi, nevertheless point to the existence of this phenomenon in Iraq, Turkey, Syria, and Jordan. Crown Colony agriculturists in Cyprus assume its existence but have despaired of identifying it with exactness. Meanwhile recent studies in the Northwest Frontier Province in Pakistan and in Egypt have concluded that widespread disguised unemployment does not in effect exist and that removal of farm workers, without substitution of machinery, education for those remaining, and other changes, would lead to decreased production.[7] Western economic theory has outlined the problem, but has done little to tell underdeveloped countries how accurately to calculate the extent of disguised unemployment, how to cure it, and more important how to put the excess peasants to work more effectively in city factories.

Further confusion has derived from a widespread assumption of the validity of Professor James Duesenberry's "demonstration effect" for underdeveloped areas. Introduced by Duesenberry as a concept applicable to industrial countries, the idea as adapted for the Middle East envisions citizens stimulated to high levels of consumption by Hollywood movies and other contact with the West. This "revolution of expectations" leads down a path studded with excessive demand for Western-made products and increasingly lavish parties and feasts (something Middle Easterners are already reputedly skilled at). It finds its end with inadequate private savings for investment and the usual dreary difficulties over balance of payments. The Cadillac sector of the culture of Saudi Arabia is often cited as evidence of the workings of this law. Turkey and Iraq also have shown evidence supporting it.

Admittedly an engaging argument, the "demonstration effect" has yet to prove itself an everlasting brake on Middle East economic growth. The high levels of private investment in many countries in recent years, the tendency of peasants to save when at all possible (usually in gold, but seldom invested), and the very real calculations which precede the launching of feasts and celebrations tend to preclude wholesale acceptance of the thesis.

In another way, however, the "demonstration effect" does have distinct relevance to the Middle East. I refer to the area's proved capacity to import, virtually overnight, policies developed in the West over centuries.[8] Labor codes copied intact from Switzerland (as was Lebanon's), social security laws, progressive taxation, and the other measures now common to industrial nations — these have since World War II been assembled like great do-it-yourself kits in almost every Middle Eastern country. Whether they can prevent the social abuses the West designed them for, and at the same time promote economic growth, is very far from proved.

On this same theme, the import of more refined Western economic theories via academic departments and classroom instruction deserves mention. No Westerner who has watched Middle Eastern professors, trained in the West, engaging in debates over, and pressing into the minds of their students, the refinements of Western price theory and model building can avoid feeling that Professor Kenneth Galbraith's conclusion about this practice in India applies equally to the Middle East: "A very much larger number of [Indian] economic leaders look for guidance to the sophisticated economic theory of the West. To be in communion with this theory is a mark of scholarly achievement.

Again, no great store is set by its adaptation to the Indian experience. As a result, an astonishing proportion of the economics that is taught and discussed in India has little relevance to Indian problems. Indeed, some of the more refined models so discussed are not notably relevant to the Western communities where they originated." [9] It is worth mentioning that to date no significant contributions to Western doctrine, or even modifications of it, have come from the Islamic-Christian Middle East, and application of the Middle East experience to Western theory is still left almost wholly to itinerant Western economists or to economists in Israel.[10]

Another refined Western technique now being tried in the Middle East is that of input-output accounting. Fairly complete tables, showing interindustry and intersectoral relations, now exist for Israel and Cyprus. Egypt is constructing a set.[11] Israel's tables are used to trace effects of investments through its economy and as a tool in economic planning. The Cyprus tables to date have proved useful as an X-ray of the island's economy in two years, 1954 and 1957, and as a measuring rod for changes during the interim. Still unproved in the Middle East, the technique is being tried for the tasks envisioned by its American designers, as a device for economic planning and as an aid in the interpretation of economic history.

Another set of sophisticated Western concepts, those related to monetary policies permitting inflationary financing of development, are also currently on trial in the Middle East. Israel since 1948 has undergone price inflation ranging between 6 per cent and 40 per cent yearly. Cyprus has inflated the island's currency at about 7 per cent yearly for a decade. Turkey has about equaled Cyprus. Lebanon and Syria, meanwhile, carried out rapid growth for a decade after 1946 while adding steadily to their gold currency backing and maintaining virtual price stability. Now Lebanon and Syria seem to be turning toward inflation. Yet Western doctrine has given the Middle East no really guaranteed postulates on the subject. Is all inflation bad? To what extent can deficit finance be engaged in, in underdeveloped countries, without pushing prices up? What cushion to increased note issue is provided by nonmonetized peasant societies? To date Western doctrine on the subject has been taken over with only minor alterations.

Another weakness of Western economic development theory lies in its failure so far to adjust its calculations to new paces of change and acceleration. Several Middle Eastern countries are now advancing net per capita incomes at rates two or three times those posted by Western nations in the nineteenth and twentieth centuries. Others are going ahead at ten times the rates of Western growth. Against this backdrop of rapid change and acceleration, Western concepts (based as they are on per capita income increases of 1 to 2 per cent yearly) become largely meaningless.

In the same connection Western theory has not adjusted its concepts to accommodate the virtually limitless technology which is now available to the underdeveloped countries of the Middle East. Assumptions based on limited technology have been understandably part of Western doctrine. But with the Western stockpile of discoveries to draw on — making it unnecessary for an Arab or Israeli to invent the telegraph or the steam engine — and with the rates of technological advance at current levels, the oversight is a serious one. The area's recent growth suggests greater capacity to import technology than was earlier believed possible.

In contrast, Western writings on the economic history of the Middle East have indeed made advances during recent years. Studies have appeared, or are in press, which cast light on economic factors in the Crusades, Islam in the seventeenth and eighteenth centuries, problems of nineteenth century Egypt.[12] So far these have avoided sweeping generalizations such as those of R. H. Tawney and Max Weber, but they have assembled and interpreted data which might permit theorizing later. More important, they are gradually illuminating, through historical method, the wellsprings of human behavior which underlie economic decision-making in the collective mind of the Middle East.

Oddly enough the only recent Marxist doctrine of economic development with widespread circulation in the Middle East has also come from the West. Produced by Professor Paul Baran, the arguments represent sophisticated refinements of the standard Marxist-Leninist forecasts.[13] They see Western impact on Eastern society as essentially destructive, a solvent for the traditional mosaic. The middle class which emerges from the confusion proves incapable of imitating its European counterpart because of too narrow markets, monopolistic trading, lack of external economies, and the rest. Instead of becoming a vehicle for social improvement, the middle class joins with the landed and trading aristocracy as exploiters of the peasants and urban masses. It takes on the worst features of both capitalism and feudalism. Ultimately the unholy trinity of this exploitation joins with overburdensome military expenditures, foreign imperialism, pernicious investment (capital flows from poorer countries to richer ones), to create an environment which beckons in trade unionism, progressive taxation, and the other Western inventions. This all feeds the ultimate and inevitable revolt of the masses. Against the tide, Baran holds, capitalist economic planning offers a frail and at best temporary reed of support.[14]

Much of Professor Baran's forecast clearly can be challenged by events in the Middle East. Vigorous middle classes have evolved in several countries and to date seem as intent

on copying their European counterpart as on being purely
"exploitive"; the role of the army allied with middle class
revolutionaries in Middle Eastern government injects a completely unexpected element onto the scene; quasi-capitalist
economic planning has made real strides in several countries;
entry of the labor movement depends on the prior establishment of factories, which in turn depend on evolution of a
relatively vigorous entrepreneurial middle class; and the
use of the term "feudalism" when referring to underdeveloped areas represents great license with historical analogy.
Yet there is enough substance to Baran's prophecies to en-
able them to compete with much of traditional Western
doctrine — particularly the highly refined versions.

The preceding observations, admittedly fragmentary,
permit several conclusions. They accent, above all, the need
for a wholesale and continuing reshaping of Western economic concepts so as to heighten their validity. For, useful
or not, these will continue to be imported so long as the
Middle East's intellectual orientation remains westward.
The young Turks, Arabs, Iranians, and Israelis must be
given a doctrinal grounding relevant to their experience and
conditions at home. Academic economics in the Middle
East cannot endure indefinitely as an essentially escapist
exercise. And the West can only lose from the disillusion
of the young economists unwilling to engage in such acro-
batics yet unequipped by study abroad to do otherwise.

Economists in the West have, moreover, an unrivaled opportunity to develop more fully, for use abroad, the measuring tools which they have contrived and applied so suc-
cessfully at home in the last quarter-century. Extension of
national income and balance of payments accounting, intersectoral measurements such as input-output, to mention only
a few, promise to give a statistical foundation on which sen-
sible conclusions in the realm of theory and policy might

be based. But more emphasis must be placed on their construction for use abroad.

Western economics also has a rare chance to go back in its arsenal to its early twentieth century and perhaps later nineteenth century concepts. The items of relevance here — institutional studies (particularly of labor and entrepreneurship), economics of the individual firm, even the writings of "nationalist" economists such as Georg Friedrich List — are many and suggestive. They have too often been neglected by Western economists in their attacks on problems of development.[15]

Western economics has, in addition, a chance to weave into its doctrine ideas and ethical concepts which will signify that it is at least aware that material advance is not all of life. Advance in net per capita income, the basis for value judgment of most Western economic writings, denotes a materialism which oddly enough is often more Marxist than capitalist. If the Western world has anything to export, it is the set of concepts, freedoms, and ideas which have shaped it. The production of goods and services has been at best a by-product of these, and material advance cannot forever have primacy as a goal in the literature.

Finally, entry of the Soviet Union into active economic endeavors in the Middle East provides Western economics a rare challenge and opportunity. Heretofore Russia has merchandised "ideas" in the area — selling its system as superior to the capitalist article — and has played down matters of material advance. But now it too has begun attempts to promote economic development in Syria, Iraq, and Egypt. Conceivably Russian advisers (and Middle Eastern officials) may soon note that the doctrinal problems plaguing Western economic theory are even more striking for Soviet theory. The latter is built, after all, on attacking capitalism first and then, in presenting therapy, prescribing much more control and compulsion than has to date proved palatable to Middle Easterners. Soviet economics clearly will need something more persuasive than the arguments of one American Marxist if it is to eclipse the Western offering. Imaginatively revised and tailored to fit Middle Eastern conditions, Western economic doctrine could become an effective element in the cold war struggle now moving into the Middle East.

# IX

## *What Can the West Offer?*

### 2. ECONOMIC POLICY AND A "POINT OF VIEW"

What has been said earlier should impress upon readers that construction of workable theory of economic development is a necessary and long-time job. The number and quality of Western economists now turning to the task make chances good that it will be done. But meanwhile their writing will be shaped by actual events in the area. Western policies toward Middle East economic development, and the "point of view" of Americans, Englishmen, and Frenchmen, will certainly, for a decade at least, eclipse in importance the theories now being built by economists. A look at several of these policies and viewpoints is illustrative.

The most important single element in Western economic policy toward the Middle East at this juncture is the promotion, by a series of means, of high levels of public and private investment within the various countries of the area. Middle Easterners have shown, since World War II, extraordinary capacity to invest at high percentages of yearly national income — over 50 per cent in Kuwait, almost 30 per cent in Iraq, Israel, and Cyprus, over 15 per cent in Lebanon and Syria, 12 per cent in Turkey. With this record of accomplishment, denoting both public and private administrative skill, the incapacity to absorb capital exhibited as recently as the early 1950's would seem to be abating.

The Middle East is showing, in short, after some halting and overpublicized false starts, remarkable skill at converting money into dams, bridges, improved topsoil, and education — even factories. The neon-lighted palaces in the desert, blue-chip investments only eight years ago, are rapidly becoming monuments to a picturesque tradition. Their obsolescence, it might be noted, has been infinitely faster than the passing of the artifacts of America's Gilded Age.

By far the greatest part of this investment has come from the Middle East's inherent skill at exploiting its relations with the Western world. For the purpose, the area's businessmen and governments have used foreign exchange reserves accumulated during Allied Army occupations in World War II, a steady flow of emigrant remittances to Cyprus and Lebanon, capital transfers from international Jewry, West Germany, and the United States government to Israel, tax-royalty and pipeline fees paid by oil companies, sale of raw materials such as wheat and cotton, economic and military assistance from the United States government. We have seen that the eastward-moving flow of funds under these auspices now totals over $2 billion yearly — over $25 each for the citizens of Turkey, Iran, Egypt, Lebanon, Syria, Iraq, and Israel.

Among the components of the $2 billion, United States economic and technical assistance is near the bottom of the list — certainly in volume, perhaps in accomplishment. Except in Turkey and Israel, and excepting investment in education in Lebanon, where satisfactory results from our economic aid investments have certainly been gained, the record to date has been inconclusive. Amounts of United States economic assistance to all the Middle East, Africa, and Greece in the thirteen years from 1 July 1945 to 1 January

1958 totaled $4.1 billion, broken down (in billions) as follows: [1]

| | |
|---|---|
| Greece | $1.4 |
| Turkey | .6 |
| Israel | .5 |
| India | .4 |
| Pakistan | .3 |
| Other (including the Arab states and Iran) | .9 |
| | $4.1 |

In recent years, United States economic assistance to Middle Eastern nations has varied between $150 and $250 million yearly. Turkey, Israel, Pakistan, and Iran have been the principal beneficiaries. Compared to grants to these nations, American aid to the Arab countries has been small.

In view of the area's recently demonstrated and constantly growing capacity to use funds intelligently, and despite the past inconclusiveness of aid expenditures, it seems reasonable that the United States should think seriously about adding to its annual economic aid commitments. A yearly sum of $400 million to $500 million does not seem unreasonable, in view of the stakes, the implications for our security, and the obvious need for more dams, bridges, and other vehicles for sustained economic growth. Still speculative, the sums envisioned are tiny when compared to the West's prospective returns on the investment.

In this context, the United States should do everything practicable to promote the flow of private investment funds into the Middle East. Except for the international oil companies (whose investment today exceeds $2 billion), the record has so far been unimpressive. The whole of Africa,

Asia, and the Middle East to date have drawn only 12 per cent of America's $38 billion private foreign investment: 68 per cent has gone into Canada and Latin America and about 15.5 per cent into Europe and European dependencies.[2] Each year American private investors put another $3 billion to work abroad, but in about these same percentages. In recent years, private investment by Americans in the Middle East has totaled less than $100 million annually, and by far the biggest part has gone to Israel. Although exact figures are unavailable, it is reasonable to assume that Middle Eastern private investment in the United States economy might well approach this figure. Kuwait's investment alone in United Kingdom and American securities probably exceeds it.

Means of implementing this proposal are elusive and complex. Recently discussed in Congress and in countless professional meetings and studies, they consist of measures such as tax relief for overseas investors, use of American farm surpluses to aid economic development programs while preventing their competition with Middle Eastern cotton and wheat exports, insurance by the United States government for part or all of funds invested abroad, and loans to American companies for the purpose.[3] United States government action alone admittedly cannot overcome political hazards, low return on capital, and the other obstacles to foreign private investment. The governor of the State Bank of Israel, for example, estimated that foreign private investors would be lucky to get 4 per cent annual return on capital in Israel in 1957.[4] Yet the United States government should constantly explore ways to increase the flow of private funds and to adjust domestic policy toward that end. If and when the investment climate in the Middle East attains markedly greater absorptive capacity for private funds, American private investors should be ready with the funds. And public policy should be ready to help, not impede, the flow.[5]

It scarcely needs mentioning here that the United States should also participate wholeheartedly in the series of measures aimed at promoting international liquidity, rising levels of trade, and bank loans for development projects in the Middle East. I refer to the various United Nations and International Bank projects and to the various "second-mortgage" lending institutions designed to take risks deemed too great for loans from the more conservative International Bank. Many of the area's economic ills (certainly not all) derive from lack of facilities such as the above. For ten years prior to 1955, for example, Egypt increased her purchases from hard currency countries in the face of dropping cotton sales to these areas. The drain on reserves undeniably helped push her toward insolvency, possibly toward barter deals with Russia. Turkey and Syria have been in similar binds in recent years.

The United States should work, furthermore, to broaden the coverage and increase the volume of investments in the Middle East by private foundations. As the London *Economist* put it recently: "The quality and scope of the aid which is being given by the voluntary agencies, and particularly by the big foundations in the Middle and Far East, in Latin America and in Africa suggest that private thousands may be given with more care than are public millions, may be adapted more easily to the problem in hand, and may even be more useful in some ways in solving it, if only because private agencies can work with more tact and frankness, and under less public pressure, than can governmental ones. And if a private project fails, its participants will not be flayed by Congressional inquiry." [6]

The biggest foundation donors to the Middle East have been the Ford, Rockefeller, and Near East foundations.

Ford has invested about $14 million in the Middle East ($12.8 million in Turkey, Iran, and the Arab countries and $1.2 million in Israel) since 1951. Rockefeller put $20 million of its capital funds into projects in Africa, the Middle East, and Asia between 1956 and 1958. Each year the Near East foundation spends about $1 million, part of which comes from America and part from the Middle East. Strung out behind the big givers are a series of smaller foundations, giving everything from money to books to heifers, mostly to private recipients. Together these grants and commodities total $10–$12 million yearly for Turkey, the Arab states, and Iran, and many times that figure for Israel.

Foundation giving has covered a broad spectrum: help to village agricultural and industrial institutes in Pakistan, funds for advisers to shape a five year plan in the same country, more than a million dollars yearly (a quarter of its operating budget) to support the American University of Beirut, funds for rural education in a series of countries, public-health medicine investments in Iraq and Egypt, aid to business training programs in Turkey, and other forms of support. While results from these investments, like those of public funds, are still inconclusive, they have unquestionably in most instances been steps in the right direction. The American private giver has maintained his protective coloration and freedom from accusations of "influence" by the United States government remarkably well. He has, moreover, tended to invest in human beings rather than in bricks and mortar.

The next element in Western policy is again obvious. The governments of the United States, Britain, and France should exert every possible effort to help the oil companies maintain the flow of westward-moving petroleum — now running at over four million barrels daily — and their payment of more than $1 billion yearly in tax-royalties to producing and transporting countries. At this juncture it is most important to maintain high levels of economic development expenditures in Iran, Iraq, Kuwait, and Egypt. Even the question of Europe's oil supply is dwarfed by this need — Europe can after all be supplied, at a price, from Western Hemisphere sources.

Toward this end, the Western governments concerned would do well to promote the particular types of diplomacy at which oil executives operating in the Middle East have become adept. Their accomplishments have, after all, been substantial. They invented the 50–50 profit split which has endured for eight tremendously profitable years; they contrived the Iran Consortium, which rescued everybody concerned from a most embarrassing impasse in 1954; they have built an exceedingly good set of personal relations, at all levels of society, in the countries where they work; their housing projects and conscious efforts to trigger economic growth in the Middle East have promoted constructive ends. The often maligned "oil diplomacy" has, I submit, been a force for good in the Middle East. And it has had less effect than it is credited with in showing up "corrupt" regimes or in distributing largesse for devious purposes. It operates, moreover, on an intellectual plane thoroughly understandable to Middle Easterners — an achievement impossible for most public aid programs.

The tenor of recent events in the Middle East suggests that the "breathing period" of the past eight years may well be nearing its end. Sharp political changes, demands for increased production by Middle East governments in face of a glutted world petroleum market, desperate efforts by Italian, Japanese, and United States "independent" oil companies (those without, or with only minor, Middle East holdings) to secure a share of the area's astoundingly low-cost crude oil, Venezuela's example in changing its tax-

royalty terms with oil companies in late 1958, efforts by
Middle Eastern governments to move the profit split from
delivery terminals in the area all the way to the gasoline
pump in Europe or America, attempts by these same governments to form a "Texas Railroad Commission" for the
Middle East — these are a few of the problems on the hori-
zon. Incredibly skilled diplomacy by oilmen, with help from
the United States government, will be needed to solve
them.

It is pointless to emphasize that Western governments
should do all in their power to promote this diplomacy.
Events will of course dictate what governments should in
fact do. Meanwhile it seems reasonable to suggest that the
governments of Britain and the United States could well in
the future forego such self-defeating actions as the conde-
scending treatment meted the admittedly difficult Iranian
government prior to Abadan, and publicly humiliating statements which evoke retaliation by Middle Eastern political
leaders.

With the Middle East facing changing agreements, competition, and world market conditions, it would seem not
unreasonable that the United States Department of Justice
likewise do its part to aid oil companies in exercising their
all-important economic and diplomatic functions. Adolph
Berle, now having come full circle on the subject, has put
the case for the companies as follows: "The United States
has chosen to regard cooperative agreements in foreign
trade as violating the American anti-trust laws and is bring-
ing action now [in 1954] to dissolve the world-wide marketing agreements alleged to exist between the great oil
companies. Few, if any, foreign nations see any sense in our
attitude. To most European countries, the doctrine of un-
restricted and unregulated international competition may
be a successful means of handling national economic prob-

lems. But they point out that even in large countries of less size — for example Great Britain, Germany or France — the national market, however substantial, is too small to permit this in most industries. Some say forthrightly that unless nations themselves are able to work together in a sort of planned economy — which they frequently are not able to do — best let the producing units themselves do the planning." [7] Berle's words may well apply even more pertinently to the Middle East oil industry in the very near future.

Underlying the West's economic policies toward Middle Eastern nations and peoples are the less definable attitudes of Americans, Englishmen, and Frenchmen which in turn shape those policies. These "points of view" express themselves in everything from State Department and ICA policy abroad to public opinion formation in newspapers and television shows at home. In aggregate they are more crucial than day-to-day policies; they shape the decision-making of the human beings involved, and improvement of them (or its opposite) will probably determine the success or failure of the West in the Middle East.

Most important of these "points of view" is a capacity to interpret events in the Middle East in terms of what is best for the peoples and countries there, rather than solely in terms of their immediate impact on Atlantic Alliance commitments in the area. Obviously the West is now locked in a real struggle with the Soviet Union in the area. But we cannot let the heat of that struggle obscure the fact that the Middle East has long proved itself a citadel of capitalism, that its economic orientation is (Syrian and Egyptian aid arrangements with the Soviet Union notwithstanding) still strongly Western. From historical example alone the United States, United Kingdom, and France can well wager that what is good for the countries of the area is also good for them.

More specifically, Englishmen, Frenchmen, and particularly Americans should abandon much of their folklore about the role of government in shaping economic growth. Conditions in the Middle East today simply will not permit investment to go on solely under private auspices. As shown earlier, percentages of funds invested by governments are growing. Between 1952 and 1958, for example, Egypt completely reversed its ratios — from 77 per cent private and 23 per cent public in the former year to 37 per cent private and 63 per cent public in the latter. Israel has invested at about this ratio for a decade. Occasioned not only by oil, population, and resource problems but also by Middle Easterners' changing attitudes toward government (including acceptance of the military dictator as entrepreneur), the phenomenon is solidly rooted in the landscape today. The West had better find ways to live with it, not compare it unfavorably with events in nineteenth century Pittsburgh or Manchester. Above all we should avoid the meaningless epithets of "socialism" and "collectivism" when referring to it.

Corollary to the above, the United States could well temper its attitude toward political "neutralism" sufficiently to permit it to deal readily with Middle Eastern countries even though they trade with, and accept economic assistance from, the Soviet Union. Neutralism, after all, was only abandoned by the United States after Pearl Harbor. Before its discard, our unwillingness to take sides had vexed European nations for a century. Middle Eastern countries with "problem" crops such as cotton and dates to dispose of are hard put to find outlets in America and England. Soviet economic and technical aid has gone almost entirely to implement projects blueprinted, oddly enough, in Syria and Egypt by Western experts employed by the International Bank or the United Nations. Our criterion should be, "Do the programs undertaken promote economic advance and generally higher living standards?" and not "Do the countries involved take a publicly anti-Soviet stance?"

Admittedly, policies resting on the above base exhibit well-defined risks — as shown graphically by the past two years' shift in the direction of Egyptian foreign trade from the West to Soviet-bloc countries. But so long as the West remains the principal outlet for Middle East oil, the bulk of trade is still westward, and the area's intellectual orientation holds toward the United States, England, France, and Germany, the chance of success outweighs that of loss. Middle Eastern students still, with few exceptions, go westward for higher education. Syrians and Egyptians are proving shrewd bargainers with the Russians, and evidence of mutual disenchantment can already be seen. The West should stand by in readiness to capitalize on the strained relationship probable as Syrian and Egyptian demands on the Soviet Union disappear into the stratosphere. It should play for the time when Russian machinations, in Iraq and elsewhere, lose their benign coloration and come into actual conflict with Arab nationalism. Despite recent setbacks odds in the competition still favor the West.

Another "viewpoint" concerns the West's need to put greater emphasis on public investment in economic development in the Middle East and less on military investment. In contrast to European recovery programs, in which economic aid far overshadowed military outlays, United States government aid to the Middle East has been weighted more than two to one on the side of arms and accompanying pacts and agreements. These have unquestionably helped maintain internal security (in Turkey, Iran, and Pakistan, for example) and have proved more palatable to United States Congresses than economic aid. But, as suggested earlier, they have not created one military force remotely useful against Russia in a jet-nuclear-weapons age. Neighboring countries feel (with some justification, moreover) that the arms will be used against them, not the Soviet Union. And, as demonstrated in Iraq, the pacts may have little appeal to revolutionary governments. A reweighting of United States aid clearly is indicated.

Next, the West, and the United States in particular, would do well in coming years to disentangle economic assistance from the requirement that threats of Soviet subversion be prerequisite for such help. To keep harping on this theme in the Middle East is absurd. We had best admit that the Soviet cold-war offensive has shifted from Central Europe eastward and that all Asian countries face an ultimate if not immediate threat. We should cease the self-defeating practice of demanding that Middle Eastern leaders stand up for a publicly pro-Western head-count, as did the otherwise admirable Eisenhower doctrine. The fate of those who have stood up is testimony.

Next, citizens of Western nations should stand willing to promote economic growth in the Middle East without expecting political tranquillity to accompany the phenomenon immediately. Occasional rereading of the history of the Western world might prove worthwhile in this respect. Political turmoil seems to accompany rapid economic growth — of the sort through which the Middle East is now going. We in the West should try to live with it and not view the occasional baying mob or flood of radio invective with clucking consternation. These are not matters to be solved, like repair of a leaky bathroom faucet, by dispatch of an occasional high-level State Department troubleshooter.

Western countries should, moreover, realize that Middle Eastern regional economic integration and cooperation, to succeed, must develop from within the area. Until this willingness comes, efforts to promote it from without, regardless how well intentioned, will probably mean little. We have seen that the United Nations' efforts to form an economic commission for the Middle East (like those long extant in Europe, Latin America, and the Far East) have proved thoroughly abortive. The Arab states have shown little competence at economic cooperation. Schemes to bring Arabs and Israelis together to harness the Jordan river and its tributaries have proved exasperatingly futile. When the nations of the area themselves begin to move toward regional integration, we should help. Meanwhile the West's best focal point for assistance in the Middle East is still the nation state.

In this same context the Western world should avoid efforts to check economic integration in the fear that political unification might follow. The "Middle Eastern question" of today differs radically from the "Eastern question" of the nineteenth century. Events in the Arab East in the next decade may well lead to a blending of economic policies in countries heretofore linked by little but a common hatred and fear of Israel. It is conceivable that economic cooperation among Arab states, even if accompanied by more political unity than now exists, might expand economic growth, aid the region in coping with problems posed by the European Common Market, and give the Arab East a position of strength and confidence which it now lacks. Accompanying arrangements might well make the lot of oil companies easier, not harder. And this same confidence might in time lead to what no Arab will accept today — economic cooperation with Israel and abandonment of fantasies associated with utterly unrealizable military conquest of the Jewish state.

To deepen its insight into these matters, the Western world should strengthen its efforts to produce "exportable" citizens who will live and work in the Middle East. And it

should work equally hard to find ways to make the experience of these "exportable" Americans, Englishmen, Frenchmen, and Germans more available to their home countries
and to the young men and women who will eventually succeed them. Though this is already a much-labored topic, a
few further observations may still be made.

Americans clearly need to improve their "point of view"
toward living in the Middle East. As businessmen, Foreign
Service officers, teachers at United States colleges and
schools, or students, they need constantly to remind themselves that their mode of living — houses, automobiles, entertainment — should parallel, as closely as they can make
them, like elements in the lives of the "middle classes" in
the countries where they dwell. To ape the living standards
of the shaikhs and pashas — which "hardship allowances"
by firms and government often permit, with resultant squads
of household servants and multi-colored station wagons —
is highly unnatural. It too often alienates the middle class
professional and business groups with whom the West has
a budding alliance. Yet for American expatriates to "go
native," as does an occasional Arabophile, and wander about
barefoot in peasant garb is equally affected. As many American families have proved, with their modest yet comfort-
able homes, European automobiles, unostentatious enter-
taining, and genuine attempts to master Arabic, Turkish, or
Persian, a productive middle way *can* be found.

A word about language study. Undeniably, far too few
Westerners make anything resembling a serious attempt to
acquire facility in Middle Eastern tongues or literary media.
This is a real indictment, particularly when one considers
that most Arabs, Turks, and Persians, still uneducated, do
not themselves employ vocabularies much in excess of 2000
words. To overtake them in numbers of commonly used
words is far from impossible, and thereby better under-

standing of the society becomes virtually inevitable. The good will engendered for the Western cause, moreover, by the Arabic-speaking Western housewife in a vegetable market or by the businessman or teacher in dealings with tradesmen, factory workers, or peasants is immeasurable. The spirit of the attempt readily offsets lapses of grammar.

But contrary to current overemphasis on the subject, language knowledge and facility are not enough. As Dean Harlan Cleveland of Syracuse University has observed, fluent arrogance is probably worse than uncommunicated arrogance. And without the "point of view," knowledge of Arabic, Persian, or Turkish does little to enhance good relations between Westerners and the Middle East. Tension has grown on Cyprus, despite rule by generations of British philhellenes, many of whom knew far better Greek than most Cypriots. Koran-quoting Americans, Frenchmen, and Englishmen have long circulated in the Middle East without leaving any residue of genuine understanding. A combination seems necessary.

Another hopeful combination is that offered by American universities and Middle Eastern governments and educational institutions. A dozen land-grant colleges now supply teaching staffs to, and training facilities in the United States for, agricultural colleges in Turkey, Iraq, Pakistan, and Iran. A group of advisers from Harvard University has helped the governments of Pakistan and Iran in economic planning. Financed in most instances by the United States government, in others by the Ford Foundation, these schemes offer long-run chances for successful collaboration.

In the short term, however, many college programs have foundered on the same shoals as struck by the Western effort generally in the Middle East — too few exportable Americans. Knowledge of plant breeding or tractor design unfortunately is not always associated with an appropriate "point of view" for life abroad. And for each counterpart of the American agriculturist in a recent popular book who revolutionized village life in an Asian country by developing better broom straw, there are a least fifty agricultural experts abroad whose technical competence is put to no effective use whatsoever. Illiterate technicians are not suitable export items for the Middle East today.

Part of the problem also lies in the government-to-government nature of the arrangements — with the usual clearances and red-tape in Washington, Teheran, Karachi, and Ankara. This deters many good men. Worse yet it hampers their effectiveness once they do go abroad. It also in effect makes land-grant college deans and presidents run employment bureaus for United States aid programs. This widening of the net has undeniably coaxed out some excellent technical experts. It has also led to the travel abroad of others who might better have stayed home — as an occasional dean, faced with staffing a thirty-man overseas team, disposes of his own marginal staff and hires others of the same ilk for the venture. The resultant crew is often only slightly better than that described by James Michener in *Return to Paradise*. Their infliction on the Middle East is undeniably an atrocity.

Despite short-run deficiencies, the college programs — particularly those privately financed and hence more flexible and selective — offer a chance for long-run improvement in the care and feeding of exportable Americans. Many of the technical experts return to teach and do research at American colleges and universities. The more sophisticated and sensitive of these will consciously — by direction of their research, analogies used in classroom teaching — focus the minds of students on problems of the Middle East and the West's role in it. The result will conceivably be an increase in the numbers of those who want to go, and indeed should go, abroad.

Corollary to this process is the increasing interest in Middle Eastern area studies in American universities. A comparatively recent phenomenon, now being tried by two state universities and several private universities, these programs acquaint students with Middle Eastern languages and problems while they are also achieving competence in traditional disciplines. The centers also attempt to promote research in the area without sacrifice of standards of quality set by regular university departments.

The latter requirement is hard to meet. Specialists in traditional fields in university departments, for example, are understandably distrustful of the area specialist whose knowledge of theory is rusty from years of life abroad and whose writing betrays what seems an impertinent lack of concern for the refinements of modern professional theories. The regional specialist meanwhile finds little meaning for his own area in the bulk of writings on underdeveloped areas now flooding the journals — compounded as they are, in most cases, of a reinterpretation of the errors of earlier writers, by authors who have either never been abroad or who at best write vignettes based on a visit of a week or two. The extent to which the mutual antagonism can be dissolved will be of academic significance as well as important to the long-run task of training exportable Americans.

In summary, the West, particularly the United States, should do all that is practicable to keep investment levels high in the Middle East. In the coming decade the most important contribution toward this end can be made by maintaining high levels of oil flows and resultant tax-royalties, emigrant remittances, and sales of cash crops such as cotton in the West. These should, and probably will, eclipse United States foreign aid — which should nevertheless be increased substantially and used to strengthen the area's social-overhead grid of highways, public-health medicine, and the rest. They will also exceed in importance United States private investment. The latter probably will not, except for investments in oil, be drawn to the Middle East in really large quantities until economic development achieves greater momentum and higher per capita incomes permit greater investment returns.

Meanwhile, and every bit as important, the West should do everything possible to build up its intellectual stockpile of knowledge and understanding of the Middle East. Several ways, outlined in preceding paragraphs, are through language training, careful selection of overseas personnel, area studies programs, more concern by traditional academic departments for underdeveloped area studies. There are certainly others, and they must be found. For the West has to find ways to know and live better with the Middle East. Given the will, understanding can result. Kipling's dictum from *One Viceroy Resigns* —

> You'll never plumb the Oriental mind
> And if you do, it won't be worth the toil —

cannot long stand as the guide to Americans in Asia.

*Notes*

# CHAPTER I

## THE MIDDLE EAST ECONOMY: PROGRESS, PROBLEMS, AND PROSPECTS

1. The best area-wide compilation is contained in the United Nations' *Economic Developments in the Middle East, 1956–57* (New York, 1958); studies by the International Bank for Reconstruction and Development have been published for Iraq, Jordan, Turkey, and Syria; national income estimates have now been prepared by the governments of Israel, Lebanon, Iraq, Egypt, Cyprus, Jordan; monographs on these have been written by Albert Badre, "The National Income of Lebanon," *Middle East Economic Papers, 1956* (Beirut, 1957), Harold Lubbell, *Israel's National Expenditures, 1950–54* (Jerusalem, 1958), K. G. Fenelon, *Iraq's National Income and Expenditure, 1950–56* (Baghdad, 1958). The *Bulletin* of the Bank of Egypt has, in recent years, set a high standard for economic reporting.

2. K. G. Fenelon, *Iraq's National Income.*

3. For a discussion of Egypt's use of accumulated balances, see Evangelos Calamitsis, "Post-War Trends in Egypt's Foreign Trade" (unpublished M.A. dissertation, Stanford University, 1955).

4. For a detailed and penetrating discussion of these see David Finnie, *Desert Enterprise* (Cambridge, Mass., 1958).

5. See below, Chapter VII.

6. See the Institute for Mediterranean Affairs, *The Palestine Refugee Problem* (New York, 1958).

7. For directions and percentages of trade, see United Nations, *Commodity Trade Statistics*, Vols. II–VI (1952–56); the most systematic analysis of the Soviet economic offensive in the Middle East is contained in R. L. Allen, *Middle Eastern Economic Relations with the Soviet Union, Eastern Europe and Mainland China* (Charlottesville, Virginia, 1958). See also Joseph S. Berliner, *Soviet Economic Aid* (New York, 1958).

8. See United Nations Relief Works Administration, *The Economic Development Projects of Syria* (Beirut, 1958).

9. Allen, *Middle Eastern Economic Relations*, pp. 21, 54.

10. United Nations, *The Development of Manufacturing Industry in Egypt, Israel and Turkey* (New York, 1958).

## CHAPTER II

HISTORICAL ANALOGIES AND MIDDLE EAST ECONOMIC DEVELOPMENT

1. See Gottfried Haberler, "Critical Observations on Some Current Notions in the Theory of Economic Development," *L'industria*, no. 2 (Milan, 1957), pp. 373–383.

2. Dean Mason has expressed his views on the subject in his lectures at Fordham University in the fall of 1958. Mason, Galbraith and Kuznets have all discussed the subject in the meetings of Economics 287 at Harvard University. Professor Everett Hagen is currently at work on a study of the pre-conditions for economic growth.

3. See Benjamin Higgins, "The 'Dualistic Theory' of Underdeveloped Areas," *Economic Development and Cultural Change*, January 1956.

4. See V. G. Simkhovich, "Hay and History," *Political Science Quarterly*, September 1913, pp. 385–403. For a more recent elaboration of a somewhat similar thesis, see E. S. Hyams, *Soils and Civilization* (London, 1952).

5. *International Affairs*, July 1957, p. 279.

6. See C. W. Cole, *Colbert and a Century of French Mercantilism* (New York, 1939).

7. Eli Heckscher, *An Economic History of Sweden* (Cambridge, Mass., 1954).

## CHAPTER III

REFLECTIONS ON ENTREPRENEURSHIP

1. The data for this essay were collected largely from several hundred interviews with businessmen in the Middle East between 1947 and 1955, interviews with businessmen in West Pakistan in 1956 and 1957, and from discussions in the Harvard Center for Middle Eastern Studies "Colloquium on Entrepreneurship in the Middle East" in 1957. Some of the conclusions were tentatively stated in my article, "Entrepreneurship: the Missing Link in the Middle East?" *Middle East Economic Papers* (Beirut, 1955). A more definitive treatment of entrepreneurship in Lebanon is now being written by Professor Yusuf Sayegh of the American University of Beirut.

2. See Ragnar Nurkse, *Problems of Capital Formation in Underdeveloped Countries* (Oxford, 1953).

3. Max Weber, *General Economic History* (New York, 1927), p. 275, defines a rational capitalist establishment as "one with capital accounting, that is, an establishment which determines its income yielding power by calculation according to the methods of modern bookkeeping and the striking of a balance."

4. For treatment of this phenomenon, see Gino Luzzatto, "Small and Great Merchants in the Italian Cities of the Renaissance," in Frederic Lane and Jelle Riemersma, *Enterprise and Secular Change* (Homewood, Illinois, 1953).

5. See Fritz Redlich, "The Business Leader as a Daimonic Figure," *American Journal of Economics and Sociology*, January 1953.

6. See Carl Kaysen, "The Social Significance of the Modern Corporation," American Economics Association, *Papers and Proceedings, 1956*; and David Lilienthal, *Big Business: A New Era* (New York, 1952).

7. Research on this topic has been conducted in Turkey by Mr. Alec P. Alexander of the University of California and in Iraq by Dr. Kathleen Langley of Harvard University.

8. For elaboration of this thesis see Khodadad Farmanfarmaian, "Social Change and Economic Behavior in Iran," *Explorations in Entrepreneurial History* (Volume 9, Cambridge, Mass., 1956–57).

9. This phenomenon has been investigated by Professor W. D. Schorger.

10. See Peter Bauer, *West African Trade* (Cambridge, 1954).

11. For elaboration of this, see Charles Issawi, "The Entrepreneur Class in the Middle East," in *Social Forces in the Middle East*, ed. S. N. Fisher (Ithaca, 1955), pp. 116–136; George Wythe, *Industry in Latin America* (New York, 1949), pp. 164, 171; *New York Times*, 7 December 1952.

12. For treatment of the contrast in the West, see Bert Hoselitz, "Entrepreneurship and Economic Growth," *Journal of Economics and Sociology*, October 1952.

13. Quoted by E. A. Bayne in *The Calculated Risk*, American Universities Field Staff Report EAB-11-'57 (Rome, 1 September 1957), p. 9.

## CHAPTER IV

### Cyprus: The "Copra-Boat" Economy

1. The author is indebted to Mr. A. C. Sedgwick for the quotation.

2. Material in this chapter has come from data provided the

author by staff members of the Crown Colony Secretariat in Nicosia and by businessmen throughout the island of Cyprus.

3. See, for example, "Economy of Cyprus Flourishing Despite Years of Insurrection," *New York Times*, 16 December 1957; and the *Cyprus Economic Review* for the years 1950–1957.

## CHAPTER V

### TURKISH LAND REFORM: AN EXPERIMENT IN MODERATION

1. The case is persuasively stated by Doreen Warriner in *Land and Poverty in the Middle East* (London, 1947).

2. The most comprehensive treatments of land reform in the Middle East are contained in the United Nations, *Progress in Land Reform* (New York, 1954) and Doreen Warriner, *Land Reform and Economic Development in the Middle East* (London, 1957).

3. Discussion of various aspects of this evolution is contained in H. A. R. Gibb and Harold Bowen, *Islamic Society and the West* (London, 1950); Helen Rivlin, "The Agricultural Policy of Muhammed Ali in Egypt" (ms. to be published in 1960 by Harvard University Press); Doreen Warriner, *Land Reform and Economic Development in the Middle East*; Afif Tannous, "Land Reform: Key to Middle East Stability and Economic Development," *Middle East Journal*, Winter 1951; Halil Inalcik, "Land Problems in Turkish History," *Muslim World*, July 1955; Saleh Haidar, "Land Problems of Iraq" (unpublished Ph.D. dissertation, London School of Economics, 1942).

4. *Middle East Economic Digest*, 30 October 1958.

5. A good outline of the conjectures on the effects of land reform is contained in William Thweatt, "The Egyptian Agrarian Reform," *Middle East Economic Papers, 1956* (Beirut, 1957).

6. Moderate land reform has also been tried in Lebanon and Iran, with little economic effect yet visible.

7. To the author's knowledge, the best accounts of Turkish land reform and the mechanization of Turkish agriculture are in an unpublished report written by R. D. Robinson to the Institute of Current World Affairs (from Trabzon, Turkey, on 15 July 1952); and in *Farm Mechanization in Turkey* (Report by a Faculty Study Committee of the University of Ankara, Ankara, 1952).

8. Government of Turkey, *Nufus Sayimi, 1927–50* (Istatistik umum Müdürlügü, Ankara, 1953).

9. Government of Turkey, 1950 *Ziraat Sayimi* (Ankara, 1953), pp. 8–11. Trans. in R. D. Robinson, *Developments Respecting Turkey, 1955–56* (New York, 1956).

10. R. D. Robinson, Report, p. 8. Mr. Robinson encountered only two instances where land commissions had seized properties of large holders.

11. Government of Turkey, 1950 *Ziraat Sayimi*, p. 11.

12. For a penetrating discussion of this phenomenon see R. D. Robinson, "Tractors in the Village — A Study in Turkey," *Journal of Farm Economics*, November 1952, pp. 451–462.

13. R. D. Robinson, "Turkey's Agrarian Revolution and the Problem of Urbanization," paper read at the meeting of the American Sociological Society, Seattle, September 1958.

14. R. D. Robinson, "Turkey's Agrarian Revolution."

## CHAPTER VI

### The New Capitalism: Oil Companies as Innovators

1. Excellent treatments of several aspects of integration are contained in David Finnie, *Desert Enterprise*, and Carleton S. Coon, "Operation Bultiste," in *Hands Across Frontiers* (Ithaca, 1955).

2. See "Oil and Social Change in the Middle East," *The Economist*, 2 July 1955.

3. James Morris, *Sultan in Oman* (New York, 1957), p. 64.

## CHAPTER VII

### Economic Planning in the Middle East

1. Parts of this essay went into a speech by the author at the Middle East Institute conference, Washington, D.C., January 1958. Proceedings of the conference were later issued under the title, *Middle East Development: Goals, Plans, and Prospects* (Washington, D.C., 1958).

2. Paul Baran, "On the Political Economy of Backwardness," *Manchester School of Economic and Social Studies*, January 1952, p. 81.

3. The best outline of Syria's economic development projects is contained in The United Nations Relief Works Administration *Quarterly Bulletin of Economic Development*, Number 15 (Beirut, 1958).

4. For discussion of this, see A. M. Martin and W. A. Lewis, "Patterns of Public Revenue and Expenditure," *Manchester School of Economic and Social Studies*, September 1956.

5. Professor Lerner's comment was made in a discussion paper

prepared for a conference on Planning in Israel held at Harvard University in May 1958.

6. The remark has been attributed on occasion both to Mr. Paul Van Zeeland and to Mr. Hjalmar Schacht.

CHAPTER VIII

WHAT CAN THE WEST OFFER? 1. ECONOMIC DOCTRINE

1. The viewpoint is expressed in popular books such as *The Ugly American* (New York, 1958) and in articles such as that by Peggy and Pierre Streit, "Close-up of the Foreign Aid Dilemma" (*New York Times Magazine*, 13 April 1958).

2. Graham Greene's *Quiet American* typifies the group.

3. P. T. Bauer, *Economic Analysis and Policy in Underdeveloped Countries* (Durham, North Carolina, 1957), p. 15.

4. David Bell, "Allocating Development Resources: Some Observations based on Pakistan Experience" (unpublished ms., Cambridge, Massachusetts, 1958); the most pertinent attacks on the problem are contained in J. Tinbergen, *The Design for Development* (Baltimore, 1958) and H. B. Chenery, *Development Policy and Programs* (Santiago, Chile, 1957, mimeographed). Professor Theodore Schultz is also studying the matter and has published tentative hypotheses in the University of Chicago *Reports*, May 1958.

5. See F. T. Moore, *The Failures of the World Bank Missions* (Santa Monica, California, 1958).

6. Charles Issawi, *Egypt in Mid-Century* (London, 1955), p. 242.

7. Studies in Pakistan were conducted in 1955–56 by Professor T. H. Wise. Those in Egypt have been made by economists from the Bank of Egypt.

8. Professor Gottfried Haberler has developed this theme in "Critical Observations on Some Current Notions in the Theory of Economic Development."

9. J. K. Galbraith, "Rival Economic Theories in India," *Foreign Affairs*, July 1958. The phenomenon is also discussed by Gunnar Myrdal in *Rich Lands and Poor* (New York, 1958).

10. Most notable are the many books and articles by Professor Alfred Bonné of the Hebrew University in Jerusalem.

11. Israel's input-output tables were made under government auspices. Those for Cyprus were made by Mr. Simos Vasiliou, statistical officer of Cyprus, working (with assistance from the author) at Harvard University. Egyptian government economists are making the tables for their country.

12. See Steven Runciman, *History of the Crusades* (Cambridge, 1951–1954); H. A. R. Gibb and Harold Bowen, *Islamic Society and the West* (London, 1957); David Landes, *Bankers and Pashas* (Cambridge, Mass., 1958); Helen Rivlin, "The Agricultural Policy of Muhammed Ali in Egypt."

13. Professor Baran has made his points in a book and at least two articles. One of these, "On the Political Economy of Backwardness," *Manchester School of Economic and Social Studies*, January 1952, contains his main arguments.

14. *Ibid.*, p. 81.

15. One notable exception to this rule is a recently published study by Frederick Harbison and I. A. Ibrahim, *Human Resources for Egyptian Enterprise* (New York, 1958).


CHAPTER IX

What Can the West Offer? 2. Economic Policy and a "Point of View"

1. *New York Times*, 7 December 1958.

2. Brendan M. Jones, "Capital Avoiding Poorest Nations," *New York Times*, 7 December 1958; See also U.S. Dept. of Commerce, *Survey of Current Business*, September 1958.

3. See "Tax Plan to Spur Investing Abroad Promised by Aide," *Wall Street Journal*, 2 December 1958, and R. F. Mikesell, *Promoting United States Private Investment Abroad* (Washington, D.C., 1957).

4. E. A. Bayne, *The Calculated Risk*, American Universities Field Service Report, September 1957.

5. A penetrating discussion of U.S. private investment abroad is contained in R. D. Robinson, "An Inquiry into Private International Investment" (unpublished ms., Cambridge, Mass., 1958).

6. "Doing Good Abroad," *The Economist*, 11 October 1958. See also parts ii and iii of the same series, in the issues for 15 November 1958 and 6 December 1958.

7. A. A. Berle, Jr., *The Twentieth Century Capitalist Revolution* (New York, 1954), pp. 122–123.

# INDEX

Abadan, 82
Abdullah el-Salem el-Sabbah, Shaikh, 2, 101
Accounting methods, Western, 108, 118, 121
Adana, 76
Africa, 5, 11, 40, 43, 125, 126, 129
Agriculture. *See* Farming
Airlines, 22, 85, 90
Al Hasa province, 21, 83, 91, 102
American University of Beirut, 41, 46, 113–114, 129
Amman, 13
Anatolia, 68
Anglo Iranian Oil Co., 88
Ankara, 77
Animal crops, 26, 27, 71, 74
Antitrust laws, U.S., 7, 131–132
Apartment houses, 21, 22, 103
Arab Development Division, Aramco (Arab Industrial Development Dept.), 83–84
Arab-Israeli War, 38, 52
Arab states: military aid to, 14; and Israel, 22–23, 24–25, 136; politics and trade, 28; entrepreneurship, 37; farming problems, 66; economic aid to, 96, 126, 129
Arabian American Oil Co. (Aramco): integration programs, 83–85, 91, 102–103
Armenians, 37, 38
Army: position of, 73; allied with middle class, 121
Asia, 5, 43, 127, 129
Ataturk, Mustapha Kemel, 69, 73, 94, 104
Atlantic Alliance, 47, 63
Azerbaijan, 10

Baghdad, 98
Bahrein, 43
Banking, 20, 34; Western theory, 114

Bankruptcy, 45
Baran, Paul, 120, 121
Bargaining, 36
Basrah, 85–86, 90, 98
Basrah Petroleum Co., 85
Bauer, Peter: quoted, 111–112
Beirut, 13, 21, 22, 38, 84
Beka'a Valley, 42
Belgium, 43
Bell, David, 113
Berle, Adolph: quoted, 131–132
Bonds, 103
Bottling plants, 51
Bridges, 22, 90
Burgan oil field, 2
Business. *See* Entrepreneurship; Industry

Canada, 127
Cape route, 27, 29
Capital: and economic growth, 6–8, 12, 16, 17; refugee resettlement needs, 13; output ratios, 19, 59; influx in Europe and Middle East compared, 20–22; and hajj to Mecca, 43–44; in Cyprus, 55, 56, 57–58; and traditional economics, 93; in Kuwait, 101; Western theories, 115; growing Middle Eastern use of, 124, 125. *See also* Investment
Capitalism: and nationalism, 21; dominant system, 28, 34, 106, 132; versus family loyalty, 39; and religion, 42–44; and Russian doctrine, 122–123
"Cartel" agreements, Israel, 45
Chambers of commerce, 41
Christianity, *See* Religions
Chukorova plain, 41, 75, 76, 107
Civil service, Iran, 99
Class structure: and Marxist doctrine, 120–121
Cleveland, Harlan, 138
Clothing, 77, 81

economic growth, 3, 5, 16, 22, 125; oil earnings, 6, 8, 130; military outlays, 9, 10; refugees in, 12, 13; population, 16; investment, 33, 46, 105, 106, 124; industry, 38, 39; land reform, 68, 73, 107; and oil companies, 81–82, 85–88, 91; economic planning, 96–98, 99, 104; and Russia, 122, 134; foundation aid, 129; military aid, 135
Iraq Development Board, 81, 97
Iraq Petroleum Co., 85, 86, 87–88, 89
Irrigation, 42, 49, 64, 67, 68, 98
Islam. See Religions
Israel: economic growth, 3, 5, 16, 17; population, 3–4, 15, 16; gifts and aid to, 6, 96, 125, 126, 127, 129; military outlays, 9; military aid to, 10, 14; trade problems, 11, 12, 22–23, 24–25, 29, 57; refugees, 13; industry in, 15; farming, 26–27; investment, 33, 105, 106, 133; entrepreneurship, 38, 44–45, 46; economic planning, 100, 105, 108; regional relations, 104, 136; income distribution, 115; and Western economic doctrine, 118
Issawi, Charles, 27, 116
Istanbul, 77, 79
Italy, 36, 43, 45, 49, 130

Japan, 8, 130
Jews, 38, 45, 125
Jezira province, 10, 41, 103, 107
Jordan, 5, 6, 12, 13, 38, 104, 105, 114, 116
Jordan River valley projects, 12, 104, 136

Kerman, 100
Khuzistan, 82, 91, 100
Kipling, Rudyard, 141
Kirkuk, 81, 87, 89, 90
Korean War, 6, 11, 38, 52, 96, 103
Kurdistan, 9
Kuwait: economic growth, 1–2, 5, 105; oil earnings, 2, 6, 8, 130;

capital, 12; integration program in, 88, 90; economic planning, 100–101, 105; investment, 104, 105, 106, 124, 127
Kuwait Oil Co., 88

Labor, 13, 32, 44, 46; Cyprus, 52–53; Turkish farm, 76; and oil companies, 81, 89, 92; disguised unemployment, 115–116; Western labor codes, 117; Marxist view, 120, 121
Laissez faire, 104, 105, 108
Land: Lebanese investment in, 22; land reform, 30, 39, 68–79; entrepreneurs' investment in, 41–42; Cyprus problem, 49, 64; problems of use and tenure, 65–68; in Iraq, 96, 97; in Pakistan, 99. See also Farming; Soil
Land commissions, Turkish, 70, 71–72, 73, 74, 75
Landlords, 39, 46, 66, 68, 69, 75, 76, 77
Landowners, 39, 66, 67, 89, 97
Language study: need for, 137–138, 141
Latin America, 5, 40, 127, 136
Leather, 23
Lebanese Contracting and Trading Co., 89
Lebanon, 42, 84, 109, 117; economic growth, 3, 4, 5, 6, 16, 22, 105, 106, 115; economic planning, 9, 104; trade problems, 11, 60; refugees in, 12, 38; population, 16; entrepreneurship, 40, 43; investment, 46, 96, 124, 125; land problems, 65, 67, 68; Lebanese in oil companies, 92; inflationary finance, 118–119
Lerner, Abba, 108
Life expectancy, 26
List, Georg Friedrich, 122
Living standards: of Americans in Middle East, 137
Loans: from Russia to Israel, 24; from oil companies, 83, 85, 87;

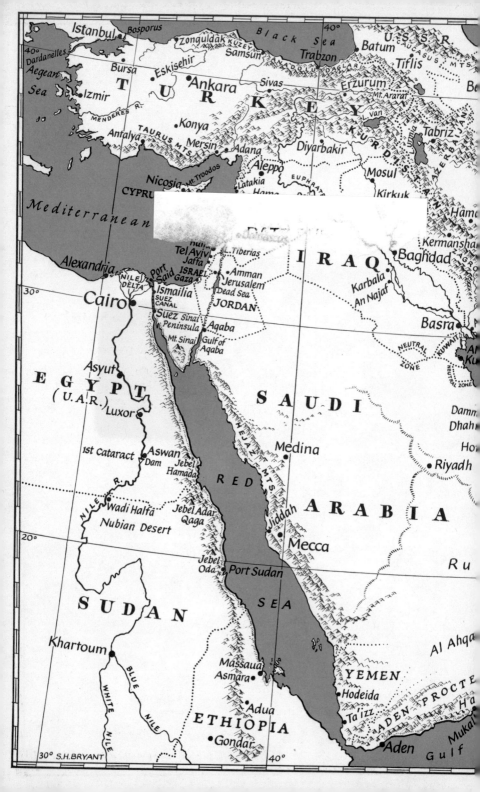